Origins of East Anglian Words & Sayings

Origins of East Anglian Words & Sayings

a

CASTELL

mini-series publication

ISBN 0 948134 66 6

CASTELL PUBLISHING © 2003
Castell Publishing Mendlesham Suffolk IP14 5RY

Sources & Acknowledgements

'Suffolk Words & Phrases' - Edward Moor 1823; 'The Vocabulary of East Anglia' - Rev. Robert Forby 2 vols. 1830; 'An Etymological and Comparative Glossery of the Dialect and Provincialisms of East Anglia' - J. G. Nall 1866; 'East Anglian Directory' - Charles Partridge M.A., F.S.A.; 'English Dialect Society' series B reprinted glossaries XVIII-XXII 1879 No XX entitled 'East Anglian Words from Spurden's supplement to Forby 1840; No XXI entitled 'Suffolk Words' from Cullum's 'History of Hawstead' 1813; 'A Glossary of Words used in East Anglia' - Walter Rye 1895; The East Anglian Daily Times 1892 - a series of 7 articles on 'Our Suffolk Speech' - principal contributors C. G. Betham and W. Wollaston Groome MD.; The East Anglian Daily Times 1924 - a series of 4 articles on 'The Suffolk Dialect'; 'Merry Suffolk' 1899 - Lois A. Fison and Mrs. Walter Thomas; 'Summut from Suffolk' reprinted from The Bury Post in Notes & Queries 6th series 1881; 'Ask the Fellow who Cuts the Hay' - George Ewart Evans; Glossary of Local Words from 'Wenhaston and Bulchamp' - Rev. J. B. Clare 1903; 'Norfolk Expressions - East Anglian Magazine XI; 'Broad Norfolk' - EAM VIII; 'Sea Words and Sea Phrases picked up along the Norfolk & Suffolk Coast' - Edward FitzGerald 1869/71; 'Peculiar Expressions & Words noted between 1881 and 1893' - Rev. C. R. Durrant; 'The Way to Wind'm' - EAM XVII; 'Words in Local Use in Suffolk & Essex' - Notes & Queries VI NS 1885/6; 'Old Essex Words' - EAMsc. 1936; 'The Rood to Framlingham?' - EAM VIII; Origins of 'Bor' - Claude Morley on Thorpe's 'Saxons in England' EAMsc. 1918; 'Broad Norfolk' published by Norfolk News; 'Suffolk Dialect 1814' EAMsc 1957; 'Dialect' - Mary Hipperson; 'Dutch and the East Anglian Dialect' - G. F. Steward C.V.O., C.B.E.; 'East Anglian Glossery' - East Anglian Magazine XVIII, XIX, XX; 'Suffolk Counting' - Madge Randell, Leslie G. Cole & Mrs. M.K.Jessup; John C. Herrington; M. Janet Becker; R. W. Hitchcock; Ida S. Critten; Mrs. R. Clover; J. Rosebrook; Wm. C. Pearson; Charles Allen; East Anglian Miscellania 1948; 1957; 1958; Notes & Queries V5 NS 1893/4; East Anglian Place-Names in Local sayings - Vivian A. Harvey; 'Pronounciation of East Anglian Locations' - Notes & Queries 1868/70; 'British Surnames' - Rev. H.Barber; 'Origins of Hall' - H.A.Harris; Suffolk Surnames of the Present Time' - A.E.Kerry; 'Ancient & Modern Surnames' - E.T.Evans, EAMsc. 1915/16; 'Elizabethan Surnames in Suffolk - Origins and Survivals' - E.T.Evans, EAMsc. 1914/15; 'East Anglian Surnames' - EAMsc. 1916; Essex Surnames' - EAMsc. 1916; Nicknames - EAMsc. 1916; 'Essex Surnames' (L.F.Matthews) - EAMag.; 'Nicknames' - Arthur H. Pye, W.E.Aldis.

Contents:

Kettleburgh.

May 22, 1814

"Dear Davy, - A was axed stound ago by Billy Pitts our 'Sessor at Mulloden (Monewden?) to make inquiration of you whether Master Bly had paid in that there money into the Bank. Billy Pitts he fare kinda unasy about it & when I see him at Church to-day he say to ma, says he, Pray have you wrot? So I kinder weft it off, & I say, says I, I han't heard from 'Squire Davy yet but I dar say I shull afore long. So pray write some lines an long me word whether the money be paid or no. I don't know what to make of our Mulloden folks, not I but somehow or other ther're allos in dibles as I' be rot if I don't begin to think some on 'em will turn up scaly at last; An as to that there fellow Bly, he grow so big an so purdy that he want to be took down a peg, but I'm glad to hare you gui't him properly at Wickham."

"I'm going to meet the Mulloden folks a Friday to go the Bounds of the town, so pray, Squire, write me word afore then, an let me know if the money be paid, that I may make Billy Pitts asy. How stammin cowd 'tis now a days! We han't no feed nowhere, an the stock run bloring about for vittels jest as if 'twas winter. You may 'pend upon't 'twill be a mortal bad sason for green Geese, an we shan't ha' no spring Cabbages afore Some fair. A clipped my ship last Teusday (List o' me, I mean Wednesday) an they scringe up their backs so nationly I'm afared they're wholly stry'd. But s' true's God 'tis a strange cowd time."

"A hant got no news to tell you, only we're all stammingly set up about that there corn bill, though some folks don't fare to like it, for they say there was a nation noise about it at Norwich last Saturday was a sennight The mob they got three effigies to imitate a Squire, an a farmer, and a miller as as strue as you're alive they hung em all upon a gibbet so folks say. Howsoever we're all quite enough here, 'cause we afre to think 'tis for our good.

"If you see that there chap Harry Jarmy pray give my sarvice to him an the same to Mr (s) Turner

"I remain Dear Squire,

Your true friend

Geo: Turner."

6

East Anglian Dialect

EAST ANGLIA has always been an isolated part of our land and its people more conservative than those of many other districts. It is therefore not surprising that its inhabitants have clung to many old words and phrases that were one time in general use. Add to these a host of true dialectical words and we have one of the most colourful and interesting dialects in the country.

How is East Anglia so different from other dialects? The words which are the basis of all phrases are derived from many foreign sources. The flatness of our coastline, our many rivers and estuaries, and the resultant accessability from the Continent have left us open to invasion from Scandinavians, Danes, Jutes, Angles, Saxons, and later, the Flemish, Dutch and French. Here these people made their first homes, draining the fenlands and plying their trades as weavers and spinners; leaving indelible marks on our dialect and adding to it a richness and liveliness.

Who among us does not enjoy a good 'mardle' at times - mardle (of French extraction) and the East Anglian for pond. The hardworking housewives of bygone days filled their buckets at the village mardle, and the men watered the cattle here, gossiping the while; now mardling and gossiping are synonymous.

Probably no part of the British Isles has had so long, so varied and so intimate a connection with the Netherlands as has East Anglia. The immigration of Flemish weavers and the Huguenots, coupled with the natural maritime associations, was greater in East Anglia than elsewhere and it would be expected that there would have been a resultant effect on the language as well as on the industry of the district. However, the borrowing of English words from the Dutch has been on a very small scale indeed and among the few dozen common words taken straight from Dutch there is a strong element of nautical terms: avast; boom; dock; freebooter; hull; marline; reef; skipper; smack; splice; swab; yacht; yawl; and other salty words such as brandy, clinker, derrick, etc.

Many of the initial emigrants from England to America came from East Anglia, led by that great Suffolk adventurer John Withrup (1588-1649) who founded Boston and became the first governor of Massachusetts. It is therefore not surprising that much of what we dismiss as American slang retains many old East Anglian colloquial expressions long disused this side of the Atlantic.

7

Silly Suffolk

"The Angles all settled in this part of England; but after a time all the acute Angles moved away to the north and the west. The obtuse Angles just stayed where they were in Suffolk!"

This prejudiced ethnographical view from a 'furrina' to Suffolk may be put in perspective by this story which shows an underlining cunning beneath the countryman's apparent simplicity:

A dealer in agricultural machinery took a beet-cutter to demonstrate to a farmer. The farmer called over one of his men and said: "Here, George, you have a go at it. Tell me what you think on it." The man, after giving the machine a jaundiced look, turned the handle and tried it with a few roots. "It's some stiff, maaster. It wholly sticks when you turn thet wheel: I fare to think it wants greasin'." "Send for Copping (the dealer); he's just across the field a-looking at that harrow," said the farmer. The verdict that 'it wants greasin'' was repeated to the dealer; but as he was a Suffolk man himself he summed up the situation in a moment. So as soon as the farmer's back was turned he slipped a shilling into the old boy's palm - six pints o' beer at that time o' day - and said to him: 'Just yew have a go at it now, bo'.' On being asked for the second time by the farmer how the machine worked, the old worker said: "It be wholly fine now, maaster. It dew go like a rick on fire."

('Ask the Fellow who Cuts the Hay' George Ewart Evans)

"I c'n rembember when I got a smack aside my lug for cloarin' through a hidge and rending my britches on a brumble."

(Norfolk dialect from Saxlingham)

East Anglian Dialect Tales
The 'Rood' to Framlingham

London visior to elderly labourer in cottage garden:
"Would you kindly direct me to Framlingham?"

Elderly labourer: "W'sartinly, sir. If you'll step inter the rood I'll show yer. Y'see that there great ellum tree stan' hinder! There's a stile jest a little fudder on. Dee yow tarn inter the fild there, an' goo kinder cornerin' acrost till y'come to an owd shod, where poor owd Billy Buckman keep his hog. Y'll see it right ahid on yer. There's a left (lifting gate) alongside o' the holl, at the fudder end o' the shod. Y'll hev to git over there an keep t'the right till y'see a kind of a hool in the hidge, where Mrs. Smith's ship (sheep) were driv throu' o' washin' day.

"A path goo from there, down to the bottom of har drift (lawk, how stout that there woman doo grow too!) If you goo up o' the drift, that'll take yer right up to har house an yards. Goo you right throu there an' keep on acrost tew midders, an' y'll come to a fild. Tha's o' barley as far as I can recollect, but lawk I can't git s'far as that now. I fare soo set fast with the rheumatics. My son-in-law he saah h'll bring me a bottle o' that there elliment what we read about in the newspaper, when he come o' Tharsday (laist o' me I mean Friday). H'is round this waah regular of a Friday forenoon about ten o'clock time, along a his booey Robbud.

"Dee yow keep t'the path alongside o' the fudder hidge, an' that'll take yer right inter the rood. Then all you ha' got to dew is t'keep right straight on t'll yer git to where Joe Garnham used to live - nut the owd gentlemen I don't mean; he live more awaah for Molstra (Marlesford) waah, paast the brick kiln.

"You'd better leave Mrs. Knights's off-buildin's on the left, an' take acrost the walks till y'come to a kind of a holler where there's three or four gret owd saller trees stan' round a hoss pond. Goo you straight on up o' the hill, an' you'll see the town right afoor yer. Y'caant g'wrong."

London visitor: "Thank you very much. I have no doubt I shall be able to find my way."

Elderly labourer (raising his voice so as to reach the departing visitor's ear): "There's a bull in that there fust midder, sir. Buut if yow keep right straight on, he 'oon't take noo notice on yer. Yow mahn't stop about, dew he may fare ugly."

Moses in a little ol' Cradle

I TOWD you larst week how that duzzy owd Pharoah were afraid them there Hebrows 'ud git tew strong for he. That wholly riled him, so he had their little owd babes, what was boys, thrown in the river Noile. One o' them Hebrow wimmin thowt she'd git the better o' that owd rascal. She wornt gooin' ter hev har child gobbled up by them narsty crocodiles, so she say to Miriam, the darter, "Goo yow across the midder and bring me a bundle o' withies, and fetch that pail o' tar. That stand agin the washus, dew that did dew."

Presently that gret mawther she come back and she say, "What are yow a-gooin' ter dew along o' they?"

"Now then," say her mother, "don't stand garpin there'. Yow can take yar little brother Aaron in the back yard and play with he, dew he'll be arskin' questions."

That wornt long afore she holller ter them ter come in. That pore woman 'ud made a cradle out o' them there withies, and there was that little owd babe a-laughin' to hisself and lyin' there as pleased as Punch. Miriam were wholly stemmed.

"Come on togither," say har mother, "we're a-gooin' ter take that down to the river and hide that in them rushes."

Time they were a-gooin' that babe niver made a mite o' sound. He wholly liked hisself in that cradle.

They hid that child in the rushes, and Miriam she stay near by to see what happen. When har mother had gorn' hoome, Miriam see Pharoah's darter comin' along ter wash harself in the river. She see suffin in the water, so she send har sarvant ter find out what that was. "Thass a Hebrow baby in a little owd cradle," say har sarvant.

"Give that ter me," said Pharoah's darter, "dew that'll git drownded. I reckon thass a noice little baby. I'll take that hoome."

Then Miriam come out o' har hidin' place and she up and say, "Dew yow want a narse for that there baby, 'cos if yow dew, I know one what 'ud suit yow well?"

She run off as fast as har legs 'ud carry har, and dew yow know she browt har mother back. When Pharoah's darter see har, she say, "What! are you back ariddy? I'll pay yow wages, dew you see arter this child for me. I'll call him Moses. That fare to be the roight name."

In coorse the woman said she'd see arter the baby, northin' 'ud please har more, so she took him to the Pallus and see arter him, and I reckon she brought him up proper to say his prayers and sarve God, and not them wicked owd idols like what them people in Egypt warshup.

Poor ould Harry

YEW may not believe this heer little ole story thet I'm a-tellun yew, but thass just as I heared that roight now. I'd just nipped out t'goo round the Loi-un (thass are loocal) when I run into ould Harry, and he look whooly done.

"Wu', boy, whassiver's a-matter," I say to him: "Yew fare whooly glum."

"Boy," he say, "if that int the rarest thing that iver happened to me," he say.

"Now whatever are yew talkun about?" I say, and all he say is, "Whoi, thass mucked me up proper, that hev."

Soo I say, "Come on heer, Harry boy, tellus whass all this heer about."

"Well," he say, "Yew know that'aire old boike of moine?"

"That I dew," I say, and I larf. (I know ould Harry and his boike all roight, arter that tale he towd us in the Loi-un larst summer. He'd just bought that then, and that has one of these'eer cycle-ommiters on the front. Dew yew know he got soo fassernated with that'aire little old tiddley-bit a-gooing round on the wheel, he was fair dorzled and couldn't keep his eyes orf that. He towd us he was a-hoppun along with his ould hid down a-watchun that goo round and round, and wallop! next he knew he was hid over 'eels in a cool-cart! But I were sayun . . .)

"WELL," he goo on, "that old boike's gone loike. This arternoon that were, I was a-doin' some sharpun in Woolwuss, and I left me boike outside loike I allus dew, then I meet auld Ted in 'aire, and he start a-tellun me how many boy-sickles he's known just lately that're bin pinched. Soo I say, "Well now I hoop moine's all roight, cos I bin and left that outside of heer larst harf'ower." "Wuh," he say, "yew'd better be arter that double quick," he say, "'cos they're a-pinchun of 'em now whooly farst! Doubt yew ont foind that'aire now, dew thass a-rummun."

"Well, I goo out thaire right farst, and I look in the street - no boike. Then I remember, and goo round the soide - and thass all roight, that little old boike's still'aire.

"Now," ould Harry goo on, and he fare a bit awk'ard heer, "I int a relijus chap, be any mort o' means, but dew yew know, I felt that thankful, that when I'm a goo-in' hoom parst the chutch, I reckon I ought to goo in 'aire and orfer up a little old prare f'r that boike bein' left unhut. Soo I leave that boi the railuns, or where them railuns useter be afore they went f'r salvedge, and I goo in f'r just a minnut.

"And dew yew know, boy," he sayter me "when I come out o' thaire and goo to fang a hold on that, moi duzzy ol' boike's gone."

Owd Bob a-Courtin'

"COURTIN' in the eighties (1880s) in the Wav'ny Valley wus a rare dairngerous job," sighed Owd Bob. "Speshly if yu were arter a little mawther in another village!"

"Bless my heart un soul - wu, yu'd on'y gotta show ya faace in the next willage un the young fellars whu lived there'd be arter yu. 'We doant want no furriners in our parish arter our gals!' they'd shout arter yu. 'Git yu back where yu b'long or yu'll git a punch on the nose!' 'Cus they warnt really so p'lite yu know, bor. Used t' swear suffun awful sometime I'm afeared.

"Come one day I tuk a fancy tu a rare nice li'l owd gal down Frazinfild (Fressingfield) way, 'un them ther boys there was out tu nab me. Fower or five on 'em cum arter me. One on 'em he say, 'Git yu hoom' tu Harlstun,' he say, 'un let our mawthers aloon.'

"This here li'l owd gal, she saw there wus a goo'en tu be some trouble and she start a-hookin' orf hum away frum me as farst as har li'l owd legs ud carry har. But I orf with my jack't und westkit and I slap 'm down on the rud, stand on top on 't, sets m'self (in fighting pose) and I say, 'Cum on m' boys, all t'gether or one at a time. Knock me orf on 't. Knock me orf on 't.

"Though I say 't whu sh'unt, I cud whooly use 'm (use his fists) in them there days. Afore yu cud say Jack Robinson I had the lot on 'm a blarin'. I whooly trimmed 'em out."

"What about the girl, Bob?" I enquired.

"Wu di'n't I tell yu she 'ud started a-hookin' orf home?" he answered. "Well as soon as she see I'd beaten the lot on 'm, she started a-sidlin' up tu me and she say, 'Cor aren't yu hully strong, boy Bob!' she say. But I say tu her, I say, 'I don't want no gals whu 'ont stand by a feller in trouble!' Then I go orf hoome and she go orf, alloon, tu har hoome, and I hint sin'r from that day tu this, and I don't want tu niither."

Mrs. Steggles in Hospital

OI niver bin ter horspital afore. Oi didn't arst ter goo. The doctor he say: 'Yow better goo, dew yow on't git rid o' them rheumatics.'

The fust noight Oi wor that hot Oi threw off a blanket. That fell on the floor. The narse she come in an' she say:

'Yow marn't dew that. Whoi didn't yow ring yar bell?'

'Bell!' Oi say, 'Oi een't sin n' bell.'

Then she shew me a cord a' hangin' on the bid wi' a knob on the end.

'Yow press that,' she say.

She pick up the blanket an' she put that on agin an' tuck that in so as Oi could hardly move.

The nex' noight that wor wholly hot agin. Oi got out o' bid an' Oi was just gooin' ter oopen the winder, when bless me if she didn't come in an' flash a torch roight in my face.

'Mrs. Steggles,' she say (she fare ter hiss at me), 'what are yow dewin' out o' yar bid? Yow marn't oopen that there winder dew yow'll wake the patients.'

'They on't wake,' Oi say ter har, 'they're all a-snorin'.'

She wor wholly in a huff that toime. Arter a bit Oi rung the bell. In she come.

'What dew yow want now? she say.

'A cuppa tea,' Oi say.

'Cuppa tea?' she say. 'Tha's nearly ha' parst foive. Yow'll ha' ter wait till then.'

'Ha' parst foive,' Oi say, 'whoi Oi een't had a mite o' sleep all noight.'

'Yes yow hev,' she say, 'yow wor farst asleep when Oi come in an hour agoo.'

'That Oi worn't,' Oi say. 'Me oies might ha' bin shut. Oi worn't asleep.'

Presently tew narses come in an' start makin' moi bid. They kep on larfin' an' talkin' about their young min.

'Oi don't pay the Health Sarvice ter hev yow tew mawthers yappin' about yar young min tergither,' Oi say, 'wakin' folk up in the middle o' the noight.'

They look at me same as if Oi wor a bit o' cats' meat. Arter we had our breakfast a parson come in dressed in blew. They call har 'Sister.'

'Mrs. Steggles,' she say, in a lah-di-dah voice, 'yow must obey the rewls.'

'Rewls,' Oi say. 'What rewls? Oi niver hard n' sin n' rewls. This een't a schule as Oi know on.'

That give har suffin ter think about. Then the doctor come. He stand at the foot o' the bid, afroide he moight catch suffin dew he come tew nare.

'How owd are yow?' he say.

'Seventy-six come March,' Oi say, 'an' Oi want ter goo hoome.'

'That on't be long afore yow goo,' he say. 'There een't much the matter. What yow want is heat.'

'Heat,' Oi say. 'Oi've had heat enuf in this here horspital.'

'Take har down to the fizzytharap room,' he say to the narse (leastways tha's what that sound loike). 'She can hev some mesardge.'

'Wha's that?' Oi say.

'They'ss rub yer,' he say larfin.

Arter he gone, they druv me in an owd chair on wheels ter the fizzy room. Niver did Oi see sech a place. They lay me on a bid and put a gret owd tin oover me loike an oven wi' oonly me hid stickin' out one end. Then they twiddle some knobs and tarn on the heat and bless me if Oi worn't layin' there bein' roosted loike a tarkey.

'Dew yow tarn me oover,' Oi holler, 'dew Oi'll be done tew much one soide.'

Then a young woman in a whoite coot come along. She move th' owd tin an' start rubbin' moi legs.

'Oi can dew that meself,' Oi say, 'or moi owd man can dew that.'

The doctor come nex' day. he say:

'Yow can goo hoome termorrer an' come as an out-patient in the amblyence.' 'What for?' Oi say.

'Cos yow want ter goo on hevin' this radio heat treatment,' he say.

'Heat,' Oi say. 'Oi can set in front o' moi foire at hoome an' git a plenty o' heat an' Oi tell yow what young man - Oi reckon moi owd gran-mother could larn yow how to cure the screws dew she wor aloive.'

'How'd she dew that?' he say.

'She wrap her joints in rid flannel,' Oi say, 'an fust she sook that in whisky. Northin' ud a-made har loi in yar oven in that there fizzy room, all of a sweat.'

'Dew yow bring me the whisky,' he say, 'an yow can hev the rid flannel.'

The duzzy fule. Imprydence! Tha's what you git in horspitals.

"Good daa to 'ee, Mrs. Potter, how are ye a-gettin' arn?"

"I'm a-doin' good-tidily, thank'ee, better'n tew or tree weeks sin'. The doctor say I fare to be on the mend; but it hev bin a bad time w' me sure."

"Ay; awd bones 'on't be young agen, I'm thinkin'; but there, 'taint so much yer aige, 'tis yer sperrut what keep ye up or let ye down."

"Ay, that be trew," says one of the group, "what be life wi'out sperrut? Nothin', in a manner o' speakin'."

"Yar farther, Mrs. Cobbold, he had it, and he lived to be ninety."

"What a man that wor.' I mind him when he come to mine arter he'd walked from Ipsich, an' tha's a good ten miles. He come to paiy a shullun he ew my ole man, and, barrin' a bit tirsty, he were as spry as a mavish and fresher'n a paigle."

Some Old East Anglian Expressions

'As smart as a carrot' - describing an overdressed woman.

Brush the stubble - to stick thorn bushes into the stubble fields to entangle the nets of night poachers.

'Them highlows o' mine du maake a duller' - (see Dialect Directory)

'Har 'ont git fudda than Wednesda' - 'She won't get further than Wednesday' - describing a person of weak intellect.

'As black as the hakes'

'All up at Harwich' - in a muddle.

'Like num-chance on horseback'

'Strappin' fine mawther' - very fine woman.

'Gret hudderen good-for-nowt' - a useless person.

'As lazy as Hall's dorg'

'An Aylsham treat' - nothing!

'The last Saturday as ever was' - last Saturday.

'He didn't ought to' - he should not have.

'I like myself very well' - I am very well satisfied with my present postion or state.

'A great sight' - a great many.

'He may do it a time or two' - once or twice.

'There was a precious site of them' - There was a great many of them.

'All along o' you' - "It is all along o' you that this happened." meaning 'it is your fault.'

'He had a stinking hide' - unpleasant smell.

'Goodly tight' - in tolerably good condition.

'I shall be on to you when I see you' - I shall ask or remind you again.

'I will nip over and see you' - I will come and see you.

'There't be' - There it is.

'Spare at the spiket and pour out at the bunghole' - Refers to someone who is mean in one way and extravagant in another.

'Down in the Shires' - Refers to any 'shire' county of England whether north or south.

The perfect example of the Norfolk use of the word 'do' is: "She don't do as she oughter do - do she wouldn't do as she do do."

Similies from the 19th Century

As wet as a *fish* - as dry as a *bone*,
As live as a *bird* - as dead as a *stone*;
As plump as a *partridge* - as poor as a *rat*,
As strong as a *horse* - as weak as a *cat*;
As hard as a *flint* - as soft as a *mole*,
As white as a *lily* - as black as a *coal*;
As plain as a *pikestaff* - as rough as a *bear*,
As tight as a *drum* - as free as the *air*;

As heavy as *lead* - as light as a *feather*,
As steady as *time* - uncertain as *weather*;
As hot as an *oven* - as cold as a *frog*,
As gay as a *lark* - as sick as a *dog*;
As slow as a *tortoise* - as swift as the *wind*,
As true as the *gospel* - as false as *mankind*;
As thin as a *herring* - as fat as a *pig*,
As proud as a *peacock* - as blithe as a *grig*;
As savage as *tigers* - as mild as a *dove*,
As stiff as a *poker* - as limp as a *glove*;
As blind as a *bat* - as deaf as a *post*,
As cool as a *cucumber* - as warm as a *toast*;
As flat as a *flounder* - as round as a *ball*,
As blunt as a *hammer* - as sharp as an *awl*;
As red as a *ferret* - as safe as the *stocks*,
As blind as a *thief* - as sly as a *fox*;
As grey as a *badger* - as green as a *parrot*,
As long as my *arm* - as short as a *carrot*;
As tame as a *rabbit* - as wild as a *hare*,
As sound as an *acorn* - as decay'd as a *pear*;
As busy as *ants* - as nimble as *goats*,
As silly as *geese* - as stinking as *stoats*;
As fresh as a *daisy* - as sweet as a *nut*,
As bright as a *ruby* - as bitter as *soot*;
As straight as an *arrow* - as crook'd as a *bow*,
As yellow as *saffron* - as black as a *sloe*;
As brittle as *glass* - as tough as a *gristle*,
As neat as my *nail* - as clean as a *whistle*;
As good as a *feast* - as bad as a *witch*,
As light as the *day* - as dark as the *pitch*;
As wide as a *river* - as deep as a *well*,
As still as a *mouse* - as loud as a *bell*;
As sure as a *gun* - as true as a *clock*,
As frail as a *primrose* - as firm as a *rock*;
As brisk as a *bee* - as dull as an *ass*,
As full as a *tick* - as solid as *brass*;
As lean as a *greyhound* - as rich as a *jew*,
And ten thousand similes - equally new.

East Anglian Counting

This story was told by an old grandfather to his granddaughter back in the 1950s:

'It appears that, whenever a sheep drover walked the sheep from Bury St. Edmunds to Ixworth and thought he could not reach his destination by nightfall, my grandfather would allow him to drive them through our gates and into the orchard.

In the morning, before the drover brought them down into the street he would count them in this fashion:

Hant	Downy	Jiggen (15)
Tant	Dominy	Hain-Jiggen
Tuthery	Dick (10)	Tain-Jiggen
Futhery	Hain-Dick	Tuther-Jiggen
Fant (5)	Tain-Dick	Futher-Jiggen
Sarny	Tuthery-Dick	Full Score (20)
Darny	Futhery-Dick	

The British Museum on being sent a copy of the above stated that such pre-Saxon Celtic sets of numerals for counting sheep are known from all over the country, particularly from Yorkshire and have even been reported from America where they were clearly taken by early English settlers. They are regarded as being among the very few survivors of the pre-Saxon Celtic speech in Britain. The nearest parallels are to be found in the Celtic languages of Wales, Cornwall and Cumbria.

Another example comes from a lady who counted when playing at a school in Mildenhall, at the end of the 19th century:

Een	Eendiff
teen	Teendiff
Tethery	Thetherdiff
Feathery	Featherdiff
Fiff (5)	Bunkin (15)
Sacrel	Eenbunkin
Acrel	Teenbunkin
Core	Thetherbunkin
deffry	Fatherbunkin
Diff (10)	Jigget (20)

The Way to Wind'm *by C. I. Cudworth*

MANY, many years ago, when signpost directions left a lot to be desired (as they still do in some isolated parts of the countryside), I met an American from 'deep in the heart of Texas' hopelessly lost 'somewhere in East Anglia', vainly trying to locate 'Wy-mond-ham'. Having shown him 'the way to Wind'm', we sat down together by the side of the road, shared our lunch, and exchanged vernacular, especially with regard to place-names.

Of course I told him the obvious ones, like Hazebro for Happisburgh, Stewkey for Stiffkey, Hunston for Hunstanton, Snets'm for Snettisham, Darsn'm for Dersingham - I didn't know so very many more myself then. But I have since gathered many more specimens of 'East Anglia as she is spoke' which I could regale my American friend if ever I met him again.

Unkindly criticism from the outer world accuses the East Anglian of vocal indolence and of being so 'afeart o' the wind' that he does not open his mouth wide enough to emit all the syllables in some of his admittedly long place-names. This is perhaps especially true of coastwise Norfolk where that old enemy the east wind seems even keener than elsewhere and where the North Sea scud can blot out even a summer landscape in a matter of minutes. Hence, perhaps, the abbreviations, but they are not confined to the coastal regions. Besides those I have mentioned one could instance Garble's'm for Garboldisham, Havilland for Haveringland (the abbreviation has now become world-famous in connection with the De Havilland aircraft firm), Thelnetham pronounced Felt'm and, perhaps, oddest of all such names, Horningsheath pronounced (and now accepted and printed as) Horringer.

Some of these places are over the border in Suffolk where the natives call Lowestoft Loostarf in much the same way as they direct you to the poostarfs (meaning a post office) and where they call Stonham Aspal St'n'm Arsp'l, Cowlinge C'lidge, and Lidgate Liggit.

According to the annonymous 'Village Schoolmaster' who wrote that minor Victorian classic *Johnny's Jaunt to the Seaside*, Johnny called Felixstowe Flaixstow, Hemingstone Hamst'n and Chelmondiston Chimpin. The same author's theory that Johnny's 'Barfull' could be equated with East Bergholt is perhaps less likely than that it stood for Bardfield, 'full' being a common abbreviation for 'field' in dialect usage, as in Wassf'l for Wattisfield and many other similar names.

'Er' is an equally widespread abbreviation (Riddl'ser for Riddlesworth is a good example) - it was also common usage in Cambridgeshire where old people still call Elsworth Elser, Boxworth Boxer and where Cromwell stationed his troops by 'Lowler Hedges' (in what we nowadays call Lolworth) to lie in wait for the college plate that never went by, on its way to 'The Other Place' and King Charles.

'Fer' is also a common abbreviation for 'ford' and I was slightly puzzled to discover that Duxford people still call their village Duxer, not Duxfer, until I remembered that there had been an earlier form 'Duxworth', still perpetuated in 'Duxer'.

Oddly enough, in the Fenland village from which my own family came, our name was always pronounced 'Cuddick', never Cudder, as one might have expected, by analogy from the village names in 'worth'.

In the Isle of Ely (which like a good many other 'isles' within these islands is no longer surrounded by water, except when the floods are out) there is a small village officially designated Little Thetford. A scientist friend of mine was once out in the fens and had to enquire his way to this place, only to be received with regretful head-shakings and protestations of ignorance. When my friend pointed to the Fenman's 'tragger' and said 'But it's painted on your cart!' enlightenment suddenly dawned and with a broad grin the Webfoot replied: 'Ow, you min Li'l Fitfer! Then whoy din yow arst for ut, bor? Whoy, yar there! Thass here!'

Which brings us to the interesting point that East Anglians (among whom we will include Fenmen, for the moment) are rather like Cockneys in that they often mispronounce their TH's for F's, with consequent baffling results to furriners, even of British extraction. I have already mentioned Felt'm for Thelnetham, which is perhaps our most original contribution to such oddities of place-name variation, but the unwary visitor must be prepared for numerous other local variants, based on the same mutation.

In the Cambridge city area there is an even more curious aberration, in which the process is reversed and F's become TH's, a peculiarity I have never met with elsewhere, although of course it may well be known to philologists. Our Cambridge baker-boy used often to declare that he was 'threezin', whilst one of my acquaintances was often accused of saying that he always enjoyed 'thresh thruit on a Thriday.'

But to get back to our place-names. Some old-time East Anglians were rather tight-lipped and inclined to neigh their words down their nostrils. It was probably this 'amiable neighing' which was responsible for the insertion of extra syllables in some place-names, such as Saxlinger'her'ham for Saxlingham, and it may even have been partly responsible for such adenoidal transmutations as Gennigal for Kenninghall and Willigub for Willingham.

Such mispronounciations and abbreviations as those detailed above are by no means confined to East Anglia, although ours are perhaps more numerous and locally celebrated than some of those 'in the shires'. Just beyond our borders, it is said that Godmanchester in Huntingdonshire is sometimes called Gumster, although it is difficult to persuade living 'Gumcestrians' to admit it, in spite of a local inscription recording a *Civic Gumcestris.* One thing is sure: the name should never be pronounced God-manchester, but Godm'n'chester (or even Gob'm'chester). Nearby St. Ives varies between Sintifes and Snoives, whilst that other saintly Huntingdonshire neighbourhood, St. Neot's, is usually called St. Neets. There is an amusing local anecdote of a native who, upon being asked his opinion on the thorny question, pondered awhile and then delivered judgement thus: 'We-e-ell, some calls it Snotes and some calls it Snowts; *I* allus calls it Sneets. Yow c'n dew wot you loike.' What one should never do, apparently, is to call the place Saint Ne-otts, any more than one should ask for Me-o-pam and De-o-pam, but always Meep'm and Deep'm - nor Stonier and Mania (for Stonea and Manea) but always Stoney and Maney.

But to return to East Anglia proper - after all, what are Hunts. or Cambs. or even the Fens themselves but border lands on the way to the heathen Mercia? Norfolk calls Horsford Hosfer and Bunwell Bunn'l, Postwick Pozzick and of course Norwich Narge (or, if you deem yourself a superior person, Nurritch) but never, never Nor-witch. I have no doubt that Ipswich is also called Ipsidge to its more elderly inhabitants; Gipswick is another ancient variant that by now is merely quaint, I fear.

Unexpectedly, Norfolk says Showld'm and not Shood'm for the place they write as Shouldham. In Wayland 'Hunderd' they say Tid'n'm for Tibbenham; they also speak of Hepper for Hepworth, Fonsit for Forncett, and just over the border in Suffolk, Netts'l for Knettishall - one would not expect the superfluous initial 'K', in any event, any more than one should pronounce both the ffs in ffolkes, no matter how great the temptation.

They do not pronounce Hargham as Harg-ham, as might be expected, but as Harf'm, which reminds one of that perennial crux of the Home Counties - how does one pronounce the name Braughing, in Essex? Brawing, Brahing, Bruffing, Brarfing, Browing, Brorfing . . . ? In East Anglia Hau and Haugh are usually pronounced Haw, as in Haughley, although you can never be sure, otherwise why is Belaugh pronounced Bela and Ashmanhaugh as Ashmano, and Sutton Hoo sometimes written Sutton Haugh?

We east (anglicise) foreign names, of course, as much as possible. Waterloo and Ostend are natually dealt with in English, and not in Flemish fashion, but what about Little Hautbois? Does one pronounce such a charmingly musical French name in musical style, as say, Little Oboe, or perhaps Little Hautboy, as Purcell would have called it? I have heard a horrid rumour that it may be called Lil Obbis, but I strongly suspect that it is more often called Hawboys, following the usual pronounciation of 'hau' in East Anglian place-names.

There is really only one way of finding out for certain; I shall have to go there and enquire, which is probably as good an excuse as any other for making yet another East Anglian jaunt. But I shall have to be careful who I ask when I get there, or I shall get that almost inevitable present-day reply - 'Sorry; I wouldn't know - I'm a stranger here myself' . . .

Of course I could go on like this for pages and pages. Why, for example, is 'burgh' sometimes pronounced 'borough' and sometimes 'burr' or 'burg', and why is Ber Street in Norwich pronounced Burr Street and not 'bar' or 'bare' to fit in with normal Norfolk usage? But I must call a halt somewhere, or I shall never get to Wymondham (sorry, Wind'm) or anywhere else. And one of these days I must go to that other Wymondham, over in Leicestershire, and ask the locals how *they* pronounce the name. Who knows? They may even call it Wy-mond-ham, out there 'in the shires'.

The way to Bunwell

"Which way to Bunwell, Jack?" asked a London gentleman of a lad on the Wymondham turnpike.

"Thaar's no Bunwell round 'ere," was the reply, and then - "You mean Bunnell! - how d'ye know my name's Jack?"

"Oh, I guessed it."

"Then guess yar way t'Bunnell" said the boy.

East Anglian Place-Names in Local Sayings

EVERY county abounds in local sayings and certainly East Anglian counties can produce their share. The difficulty, however, is to know which are of East Anglian origin and which are common to other parts of the country. To be on safe ground we may, for now, forget those concerning weather-lore, crops, home-made remedies for every ailment and indeed all other subjects of country laws and sayings, except those which are without doubt of East Anglian origin in that they all refer to places by name. I suppose it could be argued that since most of the sayings have little of good and much of ill to say about our towns and villages therefore they were coined outside of East Anglia. But that, perhaps, is only wishful thinking.

The sayings divide themselves roughly into groups according to their subject matter or form. Some, for example, are of an historical or prophetical nature. Perhaps the fear of a Napoleonic invasion is recalled in the statement:

He who England's realm would win,

Must at Weyburn's Hope begin.

The following four couplets have much in common, some being content with statements of fact and some being bold enough to venture on prophecy:

Gorleston was Gorleston ere Yarmouth began,

And will be Gorleston when Yarmouth be gone.

And this is an even more sweeping forecast:

Gorleston great one day will be,

Yarmouth buried in the sea.

Perhaps there is a tinge of irony in the lines which say that:

Caister was a city when Norwich was none

And Norwich was built with Caister stone.

And this which tells that:

Rising was a seaport,

When Lynn was but a marsh;

Now Lynn is a seaport town,

And Rising fares the worse.

and further:

Rising was. Lynn is, and Downham shall be

The greatest seaport of the three.

One wonders whether such couplets come from the more fortunate of the places mentioned or from the down-trodden, almost as if in self-defence, bringing forward some of that local pride which so many of us have for our local areas as well as our counties.

There are some sayings which leave no doubt whether their origin was within or without the place mentioned. Take the following two, for example, as a contrast:

Blessed be they who live near Potter Heigham;
Doubly blessed are they that live in it.

And compare it with this which was probably coined by a native of Kessingland who was not only prejudiced in his outlook but lacked any sense of gentle feeling!:

Between Cowhithe and merry Cossingland,
The devil shit Benacre - look where it stand!

Little better was the dismissal of this village and its inhabitants so delightfully situated on the Orwell-Stour Estuary:

Shotley Church without a steeple,
Drunken parson, wicked people.

These prejudiced views appear to have been written by those unknown writers of verse with some personal axe to grind.

MANY of our place-names have found their way into similes. *'As long as Honing Long Lane'* is a local expression and it is certainly an apt description for anything of considerable length.

The inn which is mentioned in the next description might also have been responsible for an inebriated Norfolk man hearing his own nose referred to as being *'as red as Martlesham Lion.'*

The great fire of Bungay of 1668 is recalled in the saying *'as great a rogue as burnt Bungay'* and if so charming a market town was deliberately fired none but a rogue could have been responsible.

The 'fools' at fairs of the past are remembered in the description of the man at a loss as to which way to turn as being *'like a fule at Tombland Fair.'*

It must be a long time since the tree of this simile stood but the expression *'as old as Winfarthing Oak'* has outlived it and refers back to the last relic of a large forest which covered the Diss area in the days of Alfred the Great.

But who were the 'roaring boys'? My reading has given me two references. One speaks of *'the roaring boys of Hickling who made a bonfire of their parson'* and the other the roaring boys of Pakefield *'who buried their one poor parson alive.'* Which was it? Hickling or Pakefield? Burned or buried? And what had the unfortunate cleric done to deserve either end? We will leave him, however, and look at the adjectives which have attached themselves to our place-names. *'Proud Stalham,'* which Dutt recalls as being called 'the Metropolis of Broadland,' owes its name to its position, as does also *'Sleepy Ingham'*; an old Ingham man is supposed to have put on his Sunday clothes and gone to church on Monday morning! *'Silly Sutton'* merited the name if it is really true that its people used to put their hands out of the windows to find out whether it was daylight outside or not. At *'Clever Catfield,'* in contrast, you will get the correct answer to any query. You wouldn't doubt the truth expressed in *'Raw Hepstead'* if you were there at some seasons of the year.

Some of the natives of our villages and towns have attracted to themselves various epithets, not many of them of a complimentary nature. *'Gorleston Kill-Jews'* earned their name, not because of any murderous attacks but because they were so sharp in their business dealings that even Jews starved there. Lowestoft men have acquired ('earned' seems to be the wrong term) the title *'Lowestoft pea-bellies'*, no doubt because of the use of large quantities of dried peas by the men at sea, while Walberswick has given its name, or a version of it, to the loud-mouthed man as a *'Walserwig Whisperer.'*

Perhaps of all the place-name sayings the easiest to remember, and the most fascinating, are those which link together a number of places and give to them varying characters or qualities, most of which one hopes are quite unmerited. So we are told that we must go to:

> *Beccles for a Puritan,*
> *Bungay for the Poor,*
> *Halesworth for a Drunkard,*
> *And Bliborough (Blythburgh) for a Whore.*

or to:

> *Braintree for the Pure,*
> *And Bocking for the Poor;*
> *Cogshall (Coggeshall) for a jeering town,*
> *And Kelvedon for the Boor.*

another refers to the rivalry between Braintree and neighbouring Bocking:

> *Braintree Boys, brave boys,*
> *Bocking Boys, rats;*
> *High Garret, puppy dogs,*
> *Church Street, cats.*

Perhaps Blythburgh people were no worse than those of Kelvedon, except that the originator of the rhyme couldn't think of a less offensive word to

ryhme with poor! Let's be very generous and hope so! And generous too in
our reaction to these two:

Blickling Flats, Aylsham Fliers,
Marsham Peewits and Hevingham Liars,

and:

Halvergate Hares and Reedham rats,
Southwood Swine and Cantley Cats,
Acle Asses and Moulton Mules,
Beighton Bears and Freethorpe Fules.

Finally, in your travels through East Anglia, remember that:

Gimingham, Trimingham, Knapton and Trunch,
Northrepps and Southrepps, lie all in a bunch,

and take this last word of warning:

Denton in the dale and Arborough in the dirt,
And if you go to Homersfield, your purse will get the squirt.

Here are a few more sayings, the first from Cambridgeshire:

Over Singers, Swavesey Ringers,
Bluntisham Runners, Earith Gunners,
Colne Noodles, Somersham Suckeggs,
Fenton Frogs, Pidley Pancakes,
War Boys, Wistow Lads,
Bury Creepheads, Ramsey Scabs.

Bungay was once a famous town for leather, coining the saying '*Oh, go to
Bungay and get your 'britches mended!*'
Then there were the famous men who *'went to Swaffham and worked all day
atroshin' for nawthin'*.
The following inovertive ditty was coined in Halesworth using the names of
four neighbouring villages in the Waveney valley:

'You Pulham and you Rendham
And you Mendham when you Needham.'

In the 1880s children of Creeting St. Peter attended Stowupland school.
When arguments arose the saying was heard:

Stowupland bloods, get under your tubs,
You're afraid of the Creeting Peewits.

When the many beggars who rambled about the Essex-Suffolk border
seeking relief were asked where they came from, they invariably returned the
lugubrious answer *"Saffron Walden, God help me!"* Thankfully, this would
appear to have originated from the town's motto *Deo Juvante Floremus* -

"We flourish by God's help."

Said of getting disappointing results: *'Like Will Wag of Cockley'* - who ran 20 miles to milk a cow and came home dry.

Said to anyone leaving the door open: *'You must ha bin in Sole (Southwold) church!'*

Said for something forgotten: . *'Like a Cromer man's riding light.'*

Addressed to a man who was a bit bad-tempered: *'What! Have you been to Haughley to get your back?'* No, I don't get that one either.

Amber, agates, cornelians, etc., washed up by the sea are said to be: *'Cothy (Covehithe) man's jewellery.'*

The local equivilent for 'One for me, two for yourself' was: *'A Yarmouth man's treat.'*

A person hastening to poverty is said to be: *'on the highway to Needham (Market).'* Interestingly the saying, whilst in a more overblown form, existed as long ago as 1580 when from Thomas Tusser we get 'for toiling much and spoiling more, great charge small gains or none, Soone sets thine host at Needhams shore, to craue the beggars bone.'

Bad enough you may think and a dispariging simile for Needham Market but what about this old description of Mendlesham and Creeting (which Creeting is not stated): *'Mendlesham is a lousy hole, the last place the Devil made bar Creeting.'* There seems little to justify such condemnation today.

'He's on the high-road to Melton' describes a person showing signs of insanity there being at one time a large asylum here, later St. Audrey's Hospital.

A Londoner, who had failed to recipricate the hospitality of a cousin in the village of Stonham (again, which Stonham is not stated), found when he appeared at Stonham a second time, a cold welcome and the rebuff: *'No cousin in London, no cousin at Stonham.'*

And finally:

Bungay upon the Waveney,
Wingfield and Wenhaston,
Names that sound sweet to all men,
But most to a Suffolk man;
Dennington, Orford, Aldburgh,
Wickham and Framlingham,
But the name with the thunder in it
Is the name of Saxmundham.

There's a soft whistle in Westleton,
And a sneeze that is Darsham's own,
And Halesworth has a happy sound,
And Minsmere is a moan;
But the bravest name that ever
A man could wish to meet,
Is the wildness and the wintriness
And the wind in Shingle Street.

A proud boast is Bramfield,
And Wisset's a snarling sound,
While Blythburgh has a sweeter smile
Than any place around;
But of all the names in Suffolk
The first that I would pick,
Is the one which is full of laughter,
The name of Walberswick.

by Vivian A. Harvey

East Anglian Place-name Pronounciations

Aslacton - *Aselton*
Aylsham - *Elsham*
Barwick - *Barrik*
Basingham - *Bazyng-game*
Brockdish - *Brodish*
Buckenham - *Bucknum*
Bunwell - *Bunn'l*
Caldecote - *Corket*
Cawson Woodrow - *Karson*
Chelmondiston - *Chemton*
Chillesford - *Chillfud*
Coddenham - *Coddnum*
Costessy - *Cossy*
Covehithe - *Cothy*
Cowlinge - *Cullinge or C'lidge*

Cranwich - *Cranice*
Cressingham - *Crissengim*
Cretingham - *Creetnum*
Culpho - *Cullfer*
Dallinghoo - *Dall'n-goo*
Darmsden - *Dammerson*
Debach - *Debbidge*
Debenham - *Debnum*
Deopham - *Deepum*
Dersingham - *Darsn'm*
Dunwich - *Dunnidge*
Easton Bavents - *Est'n Bev'n*
Edwardstone - *Eddist'n*
Ellough - *Ellier*
Elmsett - *Emmset*

27

Elvedon - *Elld'n*
Erpingham - *Arpyng-game*
Eyke - *Ike*
Fakenham - *Fake-num*
Falkenham - *Fork-num*
Felixstowe - *Flaixstow or Flixstow*
Forncett - *Fonsit*
Fouldon - *Fouden*
Framlingham - *Franningum*
Frostenden - *Frozend'n*
Garboldisham - *Garble's'm*
Gayton - *Gyton*
Gedding - *Giddin'*
Gipping - *Gippen*
Gooderston - *Goodson*
Gosbeck - *Gorz-brook*
Gressenham - *Gresnel*
Grimston - *Grimson*
Groton - *Grawt'n*
Halesworth - *Holser*
Happisburgh - *Hazebro*
Hardingham - *Hardengim*
Hardwick - *Haddick*
Hargham - *Harfham*
Hautboys - *Hobbos*
Haverhill - *Have-rill*
Haveringland - *Havilland*
Helmingham - *Hemmingum*
Hemingstone - *Hamst'n*
Hepwoth - *Hepper*
Herringswell - *Hornsell*
Heveningham - *Heningham*
Heveringland - *Havaland*
Hollesley - *Hosely*
Horham - *Horrum*
Horningsheath - *Horringer*
Horsford - *Hosfer*
Hoxne - *Hoxen*
Hunstanton - *Hunston*

Icklingham - *Ickegum*
Ipswich - *Ipsitch*
Ixworth - *Ixuth*
Keddington - *Ketton*
Kenninghall - *Gennigal*
Kesgrave - *Kez-grev*
Kettlebaston - *Kettlebarston*
Kettleburgh - *Kerry-brah*
Knettishall - *Nettsull*
Lawshall - *Lorz'l*
Laxfield - *Laxful*
Layham - *Lium*
Leiston - *Lay-st'n*
Leizate - *Langfer*
Letheringham - *Lethringum*
Letheringsett - *Larnsett*
Levington - *Leverton*
Lidgate - *Liggit*
Lindsey - *Linnsey*
Long Melford - *Mell-fud*
Lound - *Leund*
Lowestoft - *Low-es-toff*
Mattishall - *Ledjet*
Methwold - *Muel*
Mettingham - *Mett-en-gum*
Monewden - *Mun-ey-don*
Moulton - *Moll-t'n*
Mundford - *Munfer*
Mutford - *Mutt-fud*
Narford - *Narfer*
Naughton - *Now-t'on*
Neatishead - *Netes-shed*
Necton - *Nayton*
Nedging - *Negen*
Needham Market - *Needum*
Newbourn - *New-bonn*
Northwold - *Norrel*
Norwich - *Narge or Nurritch*
Oakley - *Ogly* (with long O)

Onehouse - *One-us*
Oulton - *Oleton*
Ousden - *Owsd'n*
Ovington - *Overton*
Pakenham - *Poik-num / Pake-num*
Pettaugh - *Petter*
Pickenham - *Picknum*
Postwick - *Pozzick*
Rattlesden - *Ratelson*
Redlingfield - *Red-'n-ful*
Rickinghall - *Rick-en-hall*
Ringshall - *Rinn-shul*
Rumburgh - *Rum-brer*
Rushall - *Rhueshall*
Saham - *Same*
Santon Downham - *Downham*
Scoulton - *Scowton*
Semer - *See-mer*
Shipmeadow - *Shipp-medder*
Shouldham - *Showld'm*
Snettisham - *Snets'm*
Southwold - *Sole or Soul*
Stanford - *Stanfer*
Stiffkey - *Stewkey*
Stoke by Nayland - *Stoke Benn-ay-lun*
Stonham Aspal - *St'n'm Arsp'l*
Stradbroke - *Strubbock*
Stratford St Andrew - *Stratt-fer*
Stratford St Mary - *Stratt-fudd*
Sturston - *Stusson*
Sudbury - *Suddbreh* (clipt as 'eh?')
Sweffling - *Swuffl'n*
Swilland - *Swillun*

Talconeston - *Tackleston*
Tannington - *Tannert'n*
Tattingstone - *Tattest'n*
Taverham - *Taberham*
Thelnetham - *Feltam* (19th century)
Thetford - *Thetfor*
Thorington - *Torrint'n*
Thrandeston - *Transt'n; Framson* (C19th)
Threxton - *Trexon*
Thrigby - *Trigby*
Thwaite - *Twaite*
Tibbenham - *Tid'n'm*
Tuddenham - *Tudd-num*
Ubbeston - *Upp-st'n*
Wacton - *Woughton*
Waldingfield - *Wonnerfeld or Wannerful*
Waldringfield - *Wonnerfel or Wunnaful*
Walsham le Willows - *Woll-sum*
Wangford - *wangfer*
Wantisden - *Worn-s'n or Wonsden*
Wattisfield - *Wassf'l*
West Bastwick - *West Barrstwick*
Westerfield - *Wesserfel*
Whelnetham - *Well Neeth-um*
Wherstead - *Wursted or Wusted*
Whixoe - *Wixer*
Willingham - *Willigub*
Witnesham - *Wittleshum*
Wordwell - *Woddle*
Worlington - *Woll-'n-t'n*
Worlingworth - *Warl-'n-wuth*
Wratting - *Ratt'n*
Wymondham - *Windham*

Ancient & Modern Surnames   *by E. T. Evans*

A prolific source on which to draw for surnames is the Register of Wills which, in Ipswich, commences in 1444. It may be taken for granted that but a minority of the names are distinctively of Suffolk; Smith or Smyth, for instance, occupies a good many lines in the calender and, in an entry in 1606 the name is spelt *Smit* (the Flemish form) to which add a terminal *e* and we have what is possibly the origin of the name that is from the verb 'to smite'. The Smith is, if anything, a smiter, and indeed the Smith's hammerman or striker is, in some parts, commonly known as a 'smiter' to this day. This prevalence of the name is no doubt due to the numbers always engaged in this handicraft ever since man first began to work with metals.

One of the earliest names in the calender of wills is **Boteler**, represented by Joane of Orford whose will was proved in 1444. Its modern form of Botler is common enough and probably expresses the origin of the name from an occupation, though it is also said to be from Botteleare in Flanders and appears in the Battle Abbey Roll as Bottelere, but in many instances it may refer to the high and more or lessed official such as waited on the Pharoah. In the *Paston Letters* the name appears as Boteler and Bottiller. The Suffolk names **Goodinge, Higham** and **Longe** also appear in the 15th century. Of these Higham is a place-name and Longe appears in Norman-French as de Longa and de Longes. It is found on the Hundred Roll and as the name of a Protestant refugee in the 17th century. The only instance of it to be found as a place-name is in the case of Longa, a small island in the Hebrides which may point to a Norse origin.

Bullinge (more celebrated as Bullen or Boleyn) is by some derived from Boulogne and is found in Norman-French as de Bolein; or it may be from Bolinnes in Flanders and phonetically the last seems the most likely. The variations in the spelling are very numerous and commence with Bolling (AS *'tribe of Boll'*) but it may however very feasibly be a form of Pullein, a diminutive of Paul. Still, in favour of a derivation from Boulogne, it may be noted that in the *Paston Letters* the name of that town is spelt in one instance Boleyn; though in another it follows the pronounciation as Boloyn. The AS *Boll* was certainly an English surname and may be found now. The name Harry **Boll** is in an inventory in the *Paston Letters* of the date, presumably, 1506. **Buckle** appears as Bockyll in the 15th century and is said to be from Boucle in Flanders. It is Bukle in a letter from Friar Brackley to John Paston in 1454. **Bayman** (Orford 1458) does not appear to survive to this day; nor is **Burgate** often met with, though a place-name. There was a family of the name at Burgate Hall near Diss for a century or two from which place it no doubt derived. It is difficult to assign an origin to **Cowper** which may be from the AS *Cuppa* 'a cup' or from this earlier period, **Goodchild** (AS *Godecild* 'Goth-soldier?'). **Marthale** looks as if it might be a spelling of Martel 'the hammer'. **Ritt** and **Rydd** connected with the German Ritter 'a rider or man-at-arms' are sparsely represented and Wolbard appears at Orford in one entry only. It may come from the AS *Wolfhard* 'a strong wolf' and, except in the near form of **Wollard**, is not now found.

Agar is derived either from 'acre', a term one applied to any enclosed or cultivated land, or from the Dutch name *Ager* derived, it would seem, from 'ag' the cutting part of a weapon i.e. the sharp edge. **Bois**, no doubt French, derives from a place in Flanders of that name. The will of Thomas Pie of Saxstead was proved in 1600. The origin of the name is a little obscure. It may have been from a nickname connected with either the magpie or the piewipe (peewit) but Barber gives the Flemish name **Pye**, which has strong claims to the original pie. **Podd** of Shotley also appeared in 1600. It may be the same as *Pott* which is Flemish, or *Bott* which is Dutch; both names mean 'a messenger'. There is also an AS name *Podda* and an Old Norse name *Bot*. Parmaine, at North Hales, is now usually **Pearmain**. It is doubtless from the Old German or Flemish meaning 'bearman', either the bear's keeper or a bear-like man. **Pillborough** may be from Pulborough, Sussex, while Robert **Posford**'s family may have acquired their name from Potsford ('Bott's ford'?) near Valley Farm, Wickham Market. In the entry of the will of Henry **Payne** of Wherstead in 1602 occurs some evidence of a nickname, he being described as 'alias White Payne' - perhaps he was an albino. His descendants may now be **Whitebread** as Payne is doubtless from the French pain. **Rudding** of Alderton would be a descendant of the AS tribe of *Hrod*; Rudd or Rutt meaning 'famous'. Rudlam contains the same root and the Dutch lam 'a lamb', hence 'famous lamb'. The name **Rope** appears at North Hales in 1600. This was also spelt Roope and is *Rupe* and *Roup* in the Dutch and Flemish. It is said to be from the Norse *Hrappr* 'a yeoman'. **Robert**, from *Ruprechr*, is doubtless allied.

William **Starke** of Wickham Market no doubt could boast an ancestor of remarkable strength. John **Starling** of Brandeston, though of bird-like form, was very likely from Esterling 'a man wise or otherwise from the East', though there was a Norse nickname *Starri*, which meant a Starling, and from this he might derive; there is also an AS *Stell*. The name of **Siggers** is from the Norse *Sigurtur* meaning 'certain of victory', and becomes the Dutch *Seegers*. **Wolton**, a well-known name is no doubt synonymous with Walton. **Woolward** of Worlingworth doubtless represents an ancestor both fierce and rapicious for they gave him the name *Wolf heard* or strong wolf - or the name may be from *Wolfward* and the modern form may be **Woollard**. Another similar name is Wollam or Woollams from the AS *Wulfman*.

Aldred is pure Saxon and means 'aged councillor', as *Aldrich* stands for aged ruler. **Crispe** is said to be a shortened form of Crispin, the cobblers' patron. **Capon** at Framlingham could be from the Flemish or Dutch *Capoen*, but it might even have an Italian origin. **Coxhedge** is probably the same as Coxhead which one authority derives from Coxyde in Belgium. **Dansforth** of Framlingham may be a corrupted form of Danesworth or 'Danes-fort'.

Hall is a most interesting word, both as a name and a dwelling. A hall is now considered a dignified mansion but was formerly little removed from a cave dwelling. One of the earliest forms of protective dwelling was to dig a hole or dry ditch and occupy the excavation. Later an improvement was made by utilising the earth thrown up out of the hole for a dwelling and making the hole or ditch a first line of defence. Both the excavation and the earth thrown out were called the *Holl*, no matter which of them was used as the dwelling, but later the earth thrown out was elaborated and built up to become the Hall, whilst the dry ditch or hole was called the Holl. The root meaning of the word is 'to hide' and Hall, Holl, Hell, hole have the same meaning. Hell is the concealed place, heled over, and men and animals crept into holes to hide, and therein they hid their treasure as a dog does this day with a bone.

Hale were 'dwellers on a slope; Aldhouse (**Aldous**) were dwellers in the 'old house (ealdhus); **Brame** and **Bramson** come from aphoroetic, a surgical term for removing anything abnoxious, and is a form of Abraham; **Minter** is a 'coiner or money-changer; **Perrot** comes from the French and means 'Little Peter'; **Ram** where it cannot refer to the animal denotes *Hram* 'a raven' and is frequently found as the raven was the crest of the Danes who over-ran England; **Tuck** means a rapier or short sword and comes from the same root as stock or stoke 'the trunk of a tree; in contrast, **Tucker** was a person occuped in one of the departments of cloth making. **Savage** comes from people who dwelt in woodlands and may or may not have been savage. **Rooke** was a nickname probably from the ancient totem or from the crest. Richard le Rooke held lands in Middlesex in the 13th century and was knight of the shire in several parliaments. **Sallowes** is most likely from the place of that name in Norfolk. **Utting** appears at Mendham and was from an old AS tribal name. It seems to come from the Norse *Udr*, German *Otte* or Flemish *Utten* and be founded on Udo 'the prosperous'. **Wyard** would at first sight seem to be the same as Whyart and Wyatt, the Flemish *Wuyts* of which the AS form is *Wiard*, the Frisian *Wiaarda* and the late Dutch *Waad* which, clipping the vowels would become Wad - given a more open sound, **Ward**, and there is a Dutch name *Waarde*. The name **Wade** might in any case come direct from *Waad*, which might be the Norse *Vathi* 'a warder' (AS *wada*). **Curtis** was fairly common in the 16th century. It is either from Cortys, a place in Belgium, or from France. Courtois means 'courteous'. Curteys is in the *Paston Letters* (1477) and it appears as an Huguenot name in Norwich in 1622. **Coleman** is assigned by Barber from 'charcoal man' but he suggests it may come from *Coll* 'a helment'. **Hurren** means 'shock-headed' a common French jibe and we find them calling that woolly-pated North American Indian tribe 'Hurons'. **Hines** means son of Hine from the Old English *Hyne* meaning 'servant. **Cohen** is a Jewish surname and those in England ashamed of their origin would call themselves **Cowen** or **Cowan.** A quick reference to origins of other present surnames: **Laflin** (from McLoughlin); **Rainbird** (from Reynberd); **Death** (De Aeth); **Disbrey** (Desborough); **Garrard** (Gerard); **Lingfield** (Longehampes); **Bone** (De Bohun); **King** (Cheyne); **Larter** (Laterre); **Downton** (Domville); **Beecham** (Beauchamp); **Gostling** (Jocelyn) and **Perry** (Pierre).

Origins & Survivals of Elizabethan Surnames
by E. T. Evans

Dowsing, a Dutch name; **Downing** and **Garnham**, the last probably from AS *Georn*, meaning 'careful warrior'.

Brome is from the Suffolk place-name. **Hasyll**, from the Dutch *Hazel*, now become **Hassall**. The old Norse *Hacon* has survived the centuries and is still found as **Haken** and was a name for kings and chieftains.

Persons named **Cook** were as numerously represented at an early period as today; this is said to derive its origin from the AS *Cue*, meaning 'sprightly' and not from a culinary occupation though in some cases it may have been the latter.

Pratt is either a place-name in France or from *Du pre* (meadow), the Flemish *Praet* having the same meaning.

Watling is another frequent survival, sometimes appearing in registers as **Wadling**; it probably signifies the son of *Wat* (Walter) or Little Walter, an AS family name.

Galle survives without the final 'e'. It would probably be derived from the Flemish *Gal* (valourous).

Cachpull has had and still has a variety of spellings; the famous Margaret spelling it **Catchpole**, as many do now, though Catchpool is also found.

A name which is not now common, but which was fairly so locally in Tudor times, is **Pymar**, which it is thought is found in only two instances today, at Kenninghall and Rushall in Norfolk. It is said by Barber to derive from Pyemoor, a place in Cambridgeshire.

Lyng or **Ling** is much more often met with then and now and is found among the names of the Protestant refugees of 1618, so it probably derives from the French or Dutch, but in some instances may be from a Norfolk place-name.

The seemingly extraordinary name of Geagafield occurs in 1558. It is probably Gagenfield which may be from the AS *Gagen*, no doubt from the Norse *Gagn* - 'gain'. This survives in the modern name **Gane**.

Bowles is met with everywhere and may have been originally a compound name meaning, say, a cheerful acquaintence from Boels in Flanders. **Barber** suggests that the out-of-the-way names occuring on the East Coast were, and are, probably corruptions of the Flemish. **Broke**, **Brooke** or **Brook** and **Brock** are said by some to be from *Brock*, a badger, which derives from the Norse *Broki*. If this is fact the name no doubt came from the crest or cognizance, the originator of the family carried on his helm, or perhaps from his successfully holding the fort, for we know that the badger is a desperate fighter when besieged in his stronghold. Others take Brook to be from Broc in Normandy. The De Brocs are found in the reign of King John. Broke is also used to denote the bearer's dwelling or place of origin; as *Atte Broke* meaning either that he lived by the brook or at a place in Norfolk.

Sometimes the occupation of a person is used as well as an ordinary family name: as "Matthew Cossett alias Tenter", as one would say "Cossett the tent-maker". **Cosset** in East Anglian phraseology means a pet and only survives now, as far as is known, as a favourite name for a cow. There is also found in one register "Popant alias Bailie" the person having probably been the manor bailiff.

The names derived from trades and callings include **Fulcher,** a falconer, often spelt **Foulger**, which appears in the registers regularly for 350 years. **Fuller**, another trade name, is also frequently represented.

Among names of common occurence is found what is now **Jennings**, formerly Gennynge, Shenning and Jannings; meaning descendents of Jan or John, no doubt from the Dutch.

Another good Suffolk name appears first as Goch, later as Gouch, and finally **Gooche.** According to Barber this is identified with *Gowk*, from the Norse *Gavkr* - a cuckoo, representing probably an ancient family cognizance or totem.

Keer is a prevalent family name in many East Coast districts and in the earlier registers appears as Care, and it has descended through a variety of spelling mutations. It would seem to have the same derivation as **Carr** (though not descendent from the Scottish name) that is, from the Norse *Kari* - the god of the winds, or perhaps *Karr* - curly-haired. **Carey** and Carrie, and the French Carre have similar origins.

A name that apparently has not survived, but for which there are many entries in the 16th and 17th centuries is Salterne, whose orgins eludes one, but it may have become **Salter**. The **Garrards** or **Garrods** have, however, increased and prospered all through the centries. The name is said to be from AS. *Gaerhead* meaning 'firm (or reliable) spear'. The **Garretts** (Norman-French *Garet* perhaps from *Gare* ('clear the way') have also prevailed exceedingly. We find some few early entries of Hastow, a name that does not survive, but which may now be represented by **Astor**, which is a Norman-French name appearing as Estur in the 12th century, but Astor is found in the Hundred Roll. Hastow may be a parish clerk's version, and the occurance of the form Estur makes one think that the East Suffolk name **Estaugh** may perhaps be thus derived. The whole may be from the Norman town L'Estre from which Barber derives the surname **Easter.**

The name Medowe or Meddowe, now **Meadows**, is of very old standing in Suffolk and is found in all classes and conditions from Lords of the Manor downwards. The local family from which Earl Manvers descends was originally known by this name, but his particular branch going to court in the 17th century changed it to Pierpont. The Suffolk representative of the senior branch (which did not go to court) is at the present day a very active young medical practitioner in East Suffolk. No one has, as far as is known, assigned any meaning to the name except a possible connection with the word 'meadow', though Barber refers to a place called Meadows in Surrey which will not do for the Suffolk family whose origin is 'wropt in mystery'. Persons were often known by the situation of their dwelling, as noticed in the case of Brooke, and as to this the name of Attwell has also been before referred to. **Attwood**, for at-the-wood or Atte-wood, is fairly common in our registes and sometimes the scribe pre-fixed an aspirate. In this connection a 15th century inscription in a certain parish church in Middlesex described the defunct as 'William Atte Heven' that being presumably his last address. A curious name which still survives is **Kinborow** sometimes extended as Kyneborrowe and Kayneborrowe (it appears once as a female christian name in the 16th century, Kinborow Pont; Pont is a Belgian place-name, now Pond). Its origin has not been certainly traced: it may be identical with Kingsburgh or Kingsbury, and of the last form there are many place-names in the country.

Kyne is also found as a family name in Suffolk in the 16th century. **Oxborrow**, still common, is from a place of that name in Norfolk. **Coppen** or **Copping**, that distinctively Suffolk name, which is from the Flemish and signifies a merchant, appears of course in a large number of entries in the registers from the Elizabethan period to the present, as does **Thorpe**, which perhaps takes next place to **Smith** or **Smyth**, the latter, by the way, being the usual ancient spelling of this name. **Warner**, from AS *Whernhere*, and **Garner** are frequent; the latter from AS meaning 'careful warrior. Another name of old origin and also fairly frequent is **Toller**, from AS *Tolere* 'a tax or toll gatherer'. The original Toller may have been the person responsible to the lord of the manor for the collection of the market tolls. He is also a German personal name and there is a place in Dorset that answers to it. There are many names met with which were those of Hugenot refugees in the early 17th century. These include Masse for Masse or **Massey**; **Mallin** or Mellin for Malignes; **Mayhew** which is said to be from the town of Mayeux, and others. The name Schotchmore, now generally **Schotchmer**, is occasionally met with. It is not Flemish as might appear from the look of it, nor has it anything to do with Scotland or a grouse moor, but is from the AS *Scotmaer* 'famous archer'. The name **Prike**, formerly Prych is Flemish and of frequent occurance at this day, but it is not known that anyone bearing it has earned the title 'illustrious' which is its meaning.

Names ending with the Danish 'by' are not numerous, but **Bunby, Bixby, Wilby** and **Gisby** or **Gisbie** and **Sainsbie (Sainsbury)** are met with; Wilby being also a local place-name and Bunby may be merely parish clerk's rendering of Bunbury, a name of some standing in the county. Gisby would appear to have come from Lincolnshire; Bixby or Bigsby being also derived from that county, though the name is best remembered as belonging to a certain East Suffolk parish clerk and gardener whose rhododendrons were 'Roads-to-Debenhams'. Thus we see how parish clerks may easily be answerable for a good deal of the corruption in the spelling of proper names. On the other hand, of course, the clergy are responsible for a large proportion of the entries; though in Tudor times very few people knew how to spell their own name and fell back on phonetics: Shakespeare for instance was in a great state of uncertainty in this respect. This name appears in various documents with nearly 30 variations not always however relating to the poet. Goultrie is a name of the 16th century which later appears as Goltie then becomes Gouttie and actually now survives, but as **Goudy, Goodey** and, perhaps, **Gooday**; though the Leigh shrimper in *Gotty and the Governor* might be an offshoot from his family. The origin is unknown. Variations in spelling are occassionally found in the course of a single entry; a case of this sort was met with, a christening, where the parents were entered as Attewode and Attwode, and the children Hatwode!

Durrant, from the French *Durand* 'enduring', and **Ward**, 'a guard': **Bendall** from the Dutch *Bendhall* or from a local place-name; **Girling**, from the AS *Gar* 'a spear', are of names the most frequent.

Among the names derived from occupations, **Carter** is common, though this may be from AS *Carda* 'a guard', not a carter as we know him. We have also Dryvar (now **Driver**) which some authorities derive from the Norman-French *De Rivers* or the Dutch personal name *Drijver*. **Maulster** and **Fisher** occur frequently, and we find **Armiger** as a surname. Does this mean the town-soldier, the local bearer of arms?

Local names like **Sudbury** might be expected. In one parish the family is described as 'alias **Game**' probably from the Dutch *Gemz*. **Potsford**, Pot from the Dutch *Bott* 'a messenger', near Wickham Market was at one time responsible for several entries. Perhaps the original owner was fished out of the Deben (Moses-like) at this point.

Grosse or **Gross** is a name as prevalent today as in the 16th century. It is said to signify big or tall, but it is perhaps also frequently applied to the circumstances of a person. **Symonds** or **Symons** is of old standing and is a contraction for Sigismond (AS. *Simond* 'victorius protector'). As might be expected in Suffolk, **Partridges** are plentiful, spelt formerly Patrich, and in some instances the name has become **Patrick**. It is found in Partriche in the Hundred Roll and also as Patrickes in 1327. It may be from Patrick, but seems more likely to have come (in these parts) from AS *Beorhtric* and Old German *Perhtric* 'illustrious ruler'. On the other hand it might have arisen from a nickname. Another not uncommon bird-name is **Sheldrake** or Sheldrick from the AS *scealdric* 'ruler's shield(?) The name **Hoare** appears to have come from the Dutch *Hoore* in which it is found in early Suffolk registers (1576) pre-fixed in one instance by the name Lodowicke which looks as if this person was the original immigrant.

Jafferson, Jeaffreson or **Jefferson** is a name sufficiently celebrated in these parts, and belongs to one of our old Suffolk adventurers. It derives no doubt from Geoffry. **Scutt** or **Skutt** is a name frequently found in the 16th century. It may be identical with **Scott** from the Dutch *Schot* or Norse *Skotti* 'an archer': one modern local form being **Skeet**. This is found as a Hugenot name in London in 1687.

Bacon is a name of ancient repute and there is a monument to a 17th century Francis Bacon in Petistree Church. The name appears to be from the Norse *Bekan*. It is found in the state papers in the time of King John. The name of **Kemp** appears early and late and is attached to a well-known family of Gissing in Norfolk which branched out all over East Anglia and into Middlesex in the 17th century. One of the family was a member for Orford which houses his monument. Its arms displays a 'garb' or wheatsheaf showing its agricultural origin. **Barber** derives the name from Campe in Normandy or from Norse *Campi* 'a champion'. **Peck** is a name found at all times in all classes and was doubtless identical with **Peche**. It may be derived from Pecq, a local name in Flanders, though some identify it with Peck from an AS personal name *Pic* 'a slasher'. Among AS names appears also **Baldry** 'the bold ruler' and, of course we have Thurkettel 'Thor's kettle' which also appears shortened to **Thurkell**, **Thurtell**, **Turtell** and **Turtill**. Also **Threadkell** from *Thrythgild* 'true value'.

Finally to show that cockneys come to the East Coast for fresh air even in the days of Queen Bess we find in the Wickham Market registers of 1558, Robert (of) London, and in the same register about the same time appears a rather puzzling name in both origin and meaning; that is Hearunto or Hearante. It may be a misreading for Hearsante, for **Harsant** is sufficiently prevelent in East Suffolk and stated to be from the AS *Hearsand* 'battle envoy', also found in the Flemish and Dutch.

Essex Surnames

The surname one still occasionally sees painted above the village shops as one travels about Essex are in many cases the same as those in the parish registers and records of the 17th and 18th centuries, and it is often possible to trace them in continuous line in many parishes from the earliest registers which date from 1538.

In the 18th century the most common surnames in the villages of the Colne valley were **Cansdale**, **Goody**, **Patten**, **Scillitoe**, **Root**, **Lay** and **Everitt**. I found on a recent visit that all of these are in evidence today (1955), in some cases following similar trades to those of their forefathers, although the miller's namesake now keeps the village bakery and the one-time wheelwright's descendant has a garage. The **Patten** family in particular have lived in the Wakes Colne area for 400 years and being in the past rather prolific have now spread all over the county.

In early records there are many variations in the spelling of names and this fact has always hindered geneologists. If you are searching parish registers don't forget to look for the name as it would have been written phonetically.

The majority of surnames are derived from trades or places. In East Anglia there are also a good proportion of Anglo-Saxon and Norse nicknames, giving rise to the number of monosyllabic surnames such as Quy, Ind and Cro. It is generally accepted that surnames began to be used in this country about AD 1000 and by the Domesday Survey both the chief and under-tenants were using them.

Through the centuries many names were altered until they bore little resemblance to the originals. Thus **Glascock** is probably derived from Glascote, a locality in Staffordshire and **Eagle** from D'Eagles or L'Aigle.

Both these are common Essex names and a Mrs. Glascock kept the original bathing huts on Southend beach when that now thriving holiday resort had less than 500 inhabitants.

Writing in 1890 H. B. Guppy gives a list of 62 surnames confined to the county of Essex. Despite the changes due to our modern way of life many of these are much in evidence today. They include the well-known business families of **Bentall**, **Marriage**, **Pertwee**, **Christy**, **Hasler**, **Playle** and **Strutt**, all of whom are frequently found in parish records.

CERTAIN names are prominent in a locality. For example in the Southend area we have **Dowsett**, **Garon**, **Gentry**, **Eve**, **Cotgrove** and **Hutley**, while in Colchester there are **Munson**, **Sparrow**, **Chopping**, **Cant** and **Eldred**. Another interesting point from Guppy's list is that five surnames derived from Essex villages remained at that time exclusive to the county, thereby giving continuity for something like 700 years. They are **Belcham**, **Hockley**, **Stock**, **Thorington** and **Wendon**.

Leaving aside the Smiths, Browns and Robinsons, the two most popular surnames of the present day that are frequently found in the records of the past are probably **Cole** and **Ellis**. Their descendants are of course now scattered throughout London and the Home Counties. The name of **Mott** is also well represented and is traceable for over 600 years. **Ravens**, **Rayners** and **Joslings** are plentiful and the old Colchester family of **Seabrook** are still living in that town.

The ancient name of **Bacon** appears all over the county and in the past there have been several knights who have held manors from the time of the Norman Conquest. **Felgate** is derived from *Felaga* who held half a hide of land in Finchingfield in the 13th century while **Folkard**, another Colchester name still in the area, came from *Folcard* an eminent Flemish scholar who was Abbot of Thorney Abbey in the 11th century.

Leatherdale is unusual, being peculiar to Essex and Suffolk and the holders of that name are all descended from Robert Lytherdale of Hasilwood (Hazelwood near Aldeburgh), Suffolk, a parish that long ago disappeared. He died in 1615 and in his will he left 'one fetherbed with goods and chattells unto Alice my well beloved wief and one payer of Maulte Querns (hand millstones) and a copper and my tramailles (fishing nets) to my sonne Francis'. This word tramaille is the original of our present word trammel, meaning a hampering influence.

The surname of **Roman** appears to have died out although at the time of

40

the hearth tax of 1662 there were families at Little Baddow, Bradwell, Thundersley, Little Totham and Shenfield. Another rare name is **Seacole**. Thomas Seacole was the first apothecary and man midwife of Southend in 1792. He came originally from Great Baddow and there does not seem to be anyone of that name now living.

The family of **Lucking** are well-known Essex worthies. At the time of the Armada, William Luckyn donated £50 to the fund collected for the defence of the county. Members of this family also served as high sheriffs in the 17th century. An important part in our village history during the 16th and 17th centuries has been played by the **Wiseman** family and the names of **Tabor**, **Spurgeon**, **Patmore**, **Lagden** (Brentwood), **Whitlock** (Halstead), **Ketley**, **Millbank** and **Pannell** are scattered throughout Essex documents.

Fairhead, a name which is mainly found in the south-east corner of the county, recalls the last case in England where the penalty of death was exacted for sheep stealing. The offence took place at Temple Farm near Rochford and Thomas Fairhead, a member of a respected Rayleigh family, was executed at Moulsham gaol on 24 March 1820. His grave in Rayleigh churchyard has long since disapppeared.

The recovery of Canvey Island from the sea has left evidence of the Dutchmen who worked on the dykes in the names of **Vandervord**, **Verlander** and **Guiver**, while the Huguenot invasion can be seen in such names as **Le Grys**, **Poupart**, **Lethullier** and **Martineau**.

Other unusual surnames include **Claryvince**, **Alp**, **Bones**, **Benniworth**, **Egg**, **Hedgethorne** and **Winterflood**. John Claryvince was a one-time rector of Chapel, while James Alp, one hundred and fifty years ago, was the blacksmith at Great Wakering and his descendants may still live in the High Street.

What has become of the descendants of Hezekiah **Hollowbread**, keeper of a Beer House at Laindon, Benjamin **Sneezum**, a baker of Grays, or Christmas **Trubshoe**, one of the first policemen at Brightlingsea?

A tombstone in St. James' Churchyard, Colchester is to Thomas **Essex**, whose descendants live in Great Oakley. He was descibed as a 'nursery and seedsman of this parish' and died in 1799.

This has only touched on the fringe of a vast and interesting subject but if you are an **Arthy**, **Basham**, **Beddall**, **Byford**, **Caton**, **Challis**, **Gowlett**, **Littlechild**, **Maskell**, **Nottage**, **Pegrum**, **Pledgare**, **Quilter**, **Ruffle**, **Scruby**, **Sorrell**, **Thurgood**, **Tillbrook** or **Wren** you are a true son of Essex.

Nicknames

NICKNAMES, a custom which, alas, appears to be waning, were once very prevalent among the inhabitants of East Anglia giving an extra colour and character to the individuals. It was a custom not just confined to the working-classes but extended to the most important people of the town. Squire and parson alike were similarly labelled.

These nicknames were frequently handed on from one generation to another and tracing their origins would prove an interesting exercise. In Beccles a family, all in printing and known as Old Potts, Young Potts and Little Potts, father, son and grandson, are descendants of a family who were manufacturers of beautiful pottery - hence the nickname. In the same town were three brothers each having a different sobriquet. There were Dar, Dillex and Double-O, whilst another branch of the family was always known as Porky. An amusing incident occured in a church on one occasion to a lad bearing this name but whose proper name was Isaiah. Porky was sitting one Sunday morning in the gallery of the church with the rest of the Sunday School children among whom was a boy slightly mentally deficient. The minister was announcing the Scripture lesson - Isaiah, chapter twenty-one, and then repeated the announcement. The startled boy was suddenly conscious that the minister was calling out a name with which he was familiar, so he excitedly called out, "Porky, Porky, the parson is a-callin' ye."

AMONGST the numerous other individuals bearing these peculiar names were Priny Ward, Doker Edwards, Drummer West, Noddy Crisp, Money and Dobbler George, Cloudy Gibbons, Tinker Beales, Blucher Rivers, Stormer Balls, Chicken Chalker, Fiddler Green, Cherry Holland, Yorkey Davey, Dilberry Pye, Honey, Scanty and Chowty Woolner, and Chitty Crickmore, the horse dealer, who in trying to sell a horse on one occasion told the prospective buyer that the animal came all the way from Glasgow in Ireland. Rat Goffin, the ferryman, had two sons Toasty and Waffity, Dreamer Flat was an athlete and Tongy Roe, the chimney sweep. Hopper Clutton earned his name by reason of the fact that instead of walking, he slouched along dragging his left leg behind him. When he was over seventy, he married a girl of eighteen who in due course produced an infant. He claimed the youngster was exceptionally bright and sent off to school at the age of three. He told how while here the teacher wrote on the board, "Children, don't play with matches. Remember the Fire of London."

"Now, does any child know anything better than that?" she enquired.

"And," said Hopper, "my little Rosie, only three, went and wrote on the blackboard, 'Children, don't spit. Remember the Flood'."

The manager of a major company in the town was called 'old Scotty' which he loved, but another 'high-up' was known as 'Blubbs' - which he *didn't* like. And then there was Pusky Cleveland, so-called because of his fondness for pea-peskets, or pea-pods, but pronounced pea-puskets. Pusky, although not quite mentally 'normal', was nevertheless possessed of a shrewd wit and humour. He took to the road and pedalled such things as bootlaces, studs and almanacs. He related how once he nearly got a permanent job. A farmer, to whom he had applied for a job, told him to take a sieve, go down to the pond, and sift all the soft water from the hard. "I carnt dew that, master," replied Pusky, "The dust might git in me eyes."

PERHAPS the most crushing retort was by a shrewd old lawyer to a rather blustering well-known miller popularly known as Robert John. He was very happy one morning in informing the lawyer that he had become the father of a son and heir.

"Well," inquired the lawyer, "what do you propose making of him?"

"Oh," replied the miller, "if he's a fool I shall make a parson of him, and if he's a rogue I shall make a lawyer of him."

"Ah," retorted the old lawyer, "and if he's half and half, I suppose you'll make a miller of him."

Odd Names from Ancient Wills

Dr. Mouse; Mouse Watson; Harty Mouse; Lady Blank; Flower Rayne; The Widow Malt; Wild Blodwell; Hagar, *who was married to* Agabas Base; Capt. Shrimps; Ambrose Spitts, *late dwelling in the Pest House*; Anne Manlove; Honor Hugge; Truelove Venus; 'Rats Jordan, *my sister*'; Florice Whopper; Fear-Not Brown; Repentance Brown; Comfort Brown; Early Roby; 'Silence, *my wife*'; Innocent Sharp; Deliverance Barrow; Purpeck Temple; Marvelous Waters; Ryce Shewte; Shooto Raven; Cough Chin; Clawson Cawson; Pleasance Goodenough; Smart Goodenough.
Surnames include:
Chink-a-Dagger; Splittimber and Ludowicke Hoore Hoore.
One testator in 1557 wills his lands "to the next of the Bludde of the Blosses."

A further selection of odd names from East Anglia past:

Ralph Pepperking Forester *(1050)*; Edward Soper, *Keeper of the Steeple 1330*; John Stilgo, *Keeper of Eye Castle 1330*; Henry & Matilda Smoky *1327*; Goodman Peg *of Westerfield 1675*; Matilda Moon *of Clare 1327*; Omendak Maria Musk; Thomasina Smallpece; Seman Tophole; Mary Washwet; Sara Ripper; Vertious Vice; Alicia Dam; Jerimiah Sharbup; William Peter Chicken *1255*; Matilda Gangz *1327*; Walter Fogseye *1327*; Thomas Gimlet *of Ipswich 1455*; Thomas Donkepot *of Gypwich (Ipswich) 1327*; Elias Chickeneye *of Bury 1327*; John Spilwind; Alexandra Pickpease; Thomas Colepeper; Bridgett Beast; John Sightright; Orlando Whistlecraft, *Thwaite weather prophet 1883.*

Dictionary of East Anglian Dialect

Abed - in bed. *"He's still abed."*

Abide - let it alone. *"will you let that abide"*

Aconite *(pronounced with long 'a')* - the flower.

A'doin' - getting well. *"He's a-doin'."*

Advertisement *(accent on the 'i')*

Afear'd - afraid.

Afore - before.

Afternoon-farmer - a lazy man. *"He's a proper afternoon farmer, he is!"*

Agin - again.

Aginst - against, in advance of - *"My pains trouble me aginst (against) the rain".*

Ain't - have not. *"I ain't finished yet."* *(see also* 'Hain't)

Aleet - four aleet - four cross-roads.

Along o' - with. *"Come along o' me".*

Always - it is his custom to do it. *"he is always doing it".*

Apple-Jack - Flap-jack; Turn-over.

A purpose - on purpose. *"He does that a purpose".*

A'ready - already.

Arger - argue.

Arede *(Essex)* - tell (to give council).

Aride *(Essex)* - attend to.

Army-Housen - almshouses.

Arrerwig (Arrawiggle) - Earwig.

A'ter - after.

Aunt Sarah - a hare.

Ax'd - I asked him. *"I ax'd he".*

Azact - that's exactly right. *"Tha's azact".*

Backen, to - to put back. *"The weather has backened the harvest."*

Balderdash - rather than talking rubbish, originally meant filthy and obscene talk

Balk - 'bout balk and French balk are terms used in ploughing. A ridge, as for potatoes. To balk up a cow is to put her head into a frame when she is being milked.

Bang - a coarse flet-cheese, originating in Suffolk and described as *"to large to swallow and too bard to bite."* *Around 1750 Suffolk Bang had such a bad name that the Admiralty condemned it as totally unfit for its warships.*

Bath *(Norfolk)* - to bath a wound, to bathe a wound.

Bats - Keys of the Ash, Sycamore, Maple, etc.

Battlings - big wood cut from hedge or tree.

Bedavilled - anything which won't work. *"wholly bedavilled".*

Bedded (Bedfast) - bedridden.

Bee-in-her-Bonnet - a crazy fancy.

Beer - of little consequence. *"He's small beer."*

Behote *(Essex)* - promised.

Bemire - admire; an old gardener sparing a plant from destruction, said *"I i'n't a-goo'n to disannul* (destroy) *that 'cause Miss Emma she do bemire it so".*

Bent - a coarse grass. *(see below)*

Bentles - name given to tract of sandy land and coarse grass at Felixstowe between the Ordnance Hotel and Landguard Fort, corresponding to the 'denes' at Yarmouth and 'links' in Scotland.

Bentlings - sandhills between Sizewell and Minsmere cliffs.

Betsy - a kettle. *"Come, boil up, Betsy!"*

Betsy and Jane - a very small piece of cheese on top of a thin slice of bread.

Betty - a fidgety child. also verb to potter - *"He only betty about now."*

Bezzle - to blunt. *"I can't sharp a scythe athowt bezzlin' it."*

Bibble - to ooze at the mouth.

Bigerty - swanky, bumptious

Big-Far'n - a self-important man.

Biggen the yard - make it bigger for ewes at lambing time.

Billy-Buster - a blusterer.

Billy-witch - July bug.

Bire *(Essex)* - confused. *"He was all of a bire."*

Bished *(Essex)* - overflowed.

Bishop (or Bishy)-Barnibee / Gowden-bug - ladybird.

Bishymeer - ant.

Blackbird with two legs - a thief.

Blare - to sing as donkeys do

Blee - water-logged ground.

Blind-sim - Blind man's bluff.

Bobjolly - a muddle, confusion or noisy disturbance.

Boisterous - Extravagant. *"She bee tew boist'rous wi' ta tey"* (with the tea).

Bone-lazy - so lazy that tiredness and fatigue seem to have perpetrated the very bones.

Bor - neighbour (Forby). A more accurate origin may date back to Saxon times for as Thorpe in his *Saxons in England* explains: *'the object of tithings was that each man should be pledge or 'borh' as well to his fellow-man as to the state for the maintenance of the public peace: that he should enjoy protection for life, honour and property himself, and be compelled to respect the life, honour and property of others: that he should have a fixed and settled dwelling where he could be found when required, where the public dues could be levied, and the public services demanded of him: lastly that, if guilty of actions that compromised the public weal or trenched upon the rights and well-being of others there might be persons* *especially appointed to bring him to justice; and if injured by others, supporters to pursue his claim and exact compensation for his wrong.'* Such a universal decree, touching every free man in the land, could not escape general recognition and thus became so deeply ingrained in the Saxon mind that the 'borh' the actual word for good fellowship has survived.

Botty - proud of. *"I am very botty about my school."*

Bowne - to 'wind' dry sprats in lieu of bloatering.

Brain - 'to brain it' means understand it.

Brank - buckwheat.

Brew - they think much of themselves. *"They don't brew any small."*

Broke - broken. *"The cup is broke".*

Brummager - one who plots but has no warrant.

Brunhustled - freckled.

Buckerhams - a horse's hocks.

Buffle - confusion.

Bumby or Bumpy - outside toilet, often in the far corner of the garden.

Bunged-up - encased, stopped-up. The cart wheels were bunged-up with mud.

Bunk - wild rabbit.

Burr - a mist round the moon. *'a far bur'* (rain), *'a near bur'* (fine weather).

Bush-Faggot - untidy, especially in referrence to disravelled hair. *"She looked like she'd bin dragged thro' a bush-faggot backards!"*

Busk - fowls lying in the sun scratching up the dust into their feathers.

Buskin - a man's leggings

Bust, on the - on the razzle-dazzle.

Butty - a clod-hopper, a country bumkin.

Cadman (Pitman) - the smallest pig in the litter.

Cammocks - The dried stems of the Wild Beaked Parsley, whence the expression *"Dry as a Cammock"*

Camp - a medieval ball game.

Camping Land - a piece of land set aside for playing Camp.

Candleless - Candlemas.

Cankers - Dogrose berries gathered for making 'Canker wine'.

Cap - to challenge.

Captivated *(Essex)* - caught.

Car' it - carry it.

Carnser (Karnser) - causeway.

Carr - small plantation (as an Ozier or Alder Carr) generally near a brook or river.

Cartshod - shed.

Ceise - to dissimulate.

Cennot - Cannot.

Centawerry - centaury *(erythroea Centaurium)*. Described by an old gardener who pronounced it a herb, not a flower, because of its medicinal properties.

Cess - a layer of stratum.

Chafe - to work calmly and steadily, not in fits and starts. A farmer to his harvesters during intense heat to steady and pull them together: *"keep chafing, men."*

Chamber - bedroom.

Chance - casual. *"He's very chance."*

Chance times - occassionaly. *"Chance times I used to meet him a-comin' home."*

Chates - food left on the plate.

Chaucers *(Essex)* - slippers.

Chisacat - *"He laughed like a chisacat."*

Chitterlings - the 'innards' of an animal.

Chobpoke - bag used by gleaners for short ears.

Chrism *(Essex)* - annointing

Chronic - irritating, worrying. *"My chilblains are wholly chronic."*

Chutch - church.

Civil - *"I do like to be treated with civil civility."*

Civil Sue - The water in which suet puddings have been boiled, which forms a good gravy to serve up with the puddings.

Clamp - an extempore and inperfect sort of brick-kiln.

Clinker - first rate article.

Clap-dish - a beggar's box. It had a movable lid, hence: *"har tong (tongue) goo like a beggar's clap-dish."*

Clapper-claw - to treat (a person) roughly.

Clappers - bird-scarers made of three pieces of wood. *"Go like the clappers."*

Clash-ma-dang - swearing, bad language.

Cleant *(pronounced as 'bent')* - cleaned.

Clereful *(Essex)* - cheerful.

Clim - a chimney imp.

Clod-hopper - a working farmer or labourer.

Clods - name given to the large thick pennies minted before 1860.

Clogwheat - a kind of wheat with havels.

Clout - a blow. *"I clouted him one."*

Clouts - old clothes.

Clunch - hard, close-grained limestone fit to be used in building but soft when first taken from the quarry.

Clutch - a clutch (nest) of eggs.

Coarse - rough, referring to the weather.

Cob - a basket.

Cob-nut - hazlenut.

Cock-farthing - a term of endearment used to a little boy.

Cockseye - mist around the moon, resembling a cockerel's eye.

Cocky *(Norfolk)* - a grating at the side of the street.

Cocky *(Suffolk)* - The Suffolk Historian, Suckling uses the word to describe a little stream of water.

Codswobbling - angry talk.

Coltishness *(Norfolk)* - a horse showing 'coltishness' showed he was a 'green' horse, that he had never been ridden or driven.

Contaking *(Essex)* - reproaching.

Cook-Eel - a bun.

Cooshies - sweets.

Cop - not very good. *"This is not much cop."*

Cop - to catch. *"Cop this."*

Cosset - to pet. *"That cat is a rare cosset"*, likes being petted.

Coverslut - a garment which is fine on the outside but shabby underneath.

Crab-eyed - with eyes protruding.

Crake - creak.

Crist - armorial shield.

Crow - one who kept watch while others stole. **Crow-Time** - *"He was left doing crowtime while the rest went after the horses."*

Cruckle - to yield under a heavy burden.

Crudden-barrow - wheelbarrow.

Cruddle - to lie close together like pigs.

Crump - blow. *"He caught him a rare crump."*

Cubby-hole - a favourite nook.

Cuckoo-Barley - barley planted late.

Cu da hell - *'good gracious!'* - *'bless my soul!'*

Cuddle - anything in a mix-up. *"They was in a pretty cuddle."*

Culch - rubbish.

Custard Aylmagne *(Essex)* - custard batter with eggs, raisins and spices.

Cyprus cat - tabby cat.

Dabster - a person clever at a particular art or occupation. *"My, you're a dabster at that!"*

Dag - dew, sea mist.

Darb - to daub.

Dardledumdue - a person without energy or notion of work.

Dark-hour - a little later than dusk hour. *"I have no moe to say if you axe me till Dark hour."*

Darnicks - fingerless hedging gloves.

Deaf - *"as deaf as a beetle"; "as deaf as a pust* (post)*."*

Deave - to dip a pail into water.

Dew - if you do. *"Don't go, dew you'll hart yerself"* - don't go: if you do, you will hurt yourself.

Dew-drink - first allowance of beer to harvesters before they begin their day's work.

Dick - very smart. *"right up to the dick"*

Dickey - donkey.

Didall - triangular-shaped ditching tool.

Diddy - secret.

Didicoys - peg sellers.

Di-do - false story.

Dilch - swindle, steal by cutting.

Dillie - Trailer *(Wickham Market area)*

Disannul - destroy

Discern - to see. *"I discarned him a-coming across the field."*

Dishabilly - dirty and stripped for work. *"I was all in my dishabilly."*

Dither, all of a - shaking with fright.

Doddy muffle - a little mouthful.

Dodman /Hodmandod / Hodmedod - snail.

Dog-in-a-basket - roly-poly pudding.

Doke - hollow, as in the impression left by the head on a pillow.

Doller - from Dutch *Dollen* to act foolishly or crazily or to frolic. *"Howd yer doller"* said to a group of arguing and shouting children.

Dominoses - the game dominoes.

Done - nonplussed, disappointed. *"He wus wholly done."*

Doom *(Essex)* - Day of Judgement

Dorr *(Cambridgeshire)* - cockchafers in Cambridgeshire are called Midsummer dorrs.

Dorzle - bewildered. *"He was wholly dorzled."*. Also apppears to describe an unsatisfactory piece of mowing as an old man said: *"I cut some, covered some and dorzled some."*

Dosser - basket.

Dot and Go (or carry) One - said of a man who shuffles in his walk.

Dove-Cotes *(Essex)* - hair-nets.

Dow *(rhymes with 'low')* - to lop off a tree's branches.

Dravely Day - showery.

Draw-latching - walk slowly, dawdle. *'I jes seen owd Tom draw-latching up the road.'*

Driftway - an enclosed strip of land forming a cartway or driving-way to the more distant lands on a farm.

Drive it off - put it off. *"I should a went today, but I dref it off till Tuesday."*

Droll - to put off, amuse with excuses.

Drove - a wide path or way over flat or fenny lands, along which cattle are usually driven. It is often distinguished as *first* drove, *middle* drove, *further* drove, etc.

Drug - vehicle used for carting trees.

Duddle-up - to cover with clothes.

Du it don't matter - it doesn't matter.

Dummy oit - deaf and dumb person.

Dunted - dazed, stupified. *"You have been pooring all day over that book; don't you feel dunted?"*.

Durst - No man dare go. *"No man durst go."*

Dutfin - a horse's bridle.

Duzzy - stupid. adjective of annoyance. *"You duzzy owd (old) fool."*

Dwile - a house cloth.

Dwinge - shrivel, shrink.

Edication - education.

Elem - Elm.

Elevenses - break for refreshments around mid-morning.

Encheson *(Essex)* - a reason, cause.

Enow - enough, used only in plural: *"I 'ad enow nuts, but not enow meat."*

Even and even - improvident. *"Thai'll nivva dew; thai mak' even and even."* - i.e. live from hand to mouth.

Executed - exercised.

Familiar - agreeable. *"He's a very familiar gentleman."*

Fardel *(Essex)* - parcel.

Fare - seem or feel. An old woman shown an uncomplimentary photograph of herself exclaimed *"I don't mind how I look, I know how I fare."*

Farewell - goodbye.

Fawters *(Essex)* - doers.

Feft - to persuade.

Fence - defend, protect. *"My mackintosh 'ont fence no more."*

Feume *(Essex)* - dirt.

Filand - a tract of unenclosed arable land.

Fil-gear - gear or harness of a leading carthorse *(see filler or thiller)*.

Filler (Thiller) - the horse, usually old, placid and past his ploughing days, which was placed between the shafts and remained there after the trace-horses had been removed.

Flack - to hang loose.

Flacket - shake - flacketting the tablecloth.

Flags - turf.

Flash - to cut hedges.

Fleet (Flet) - shallow (dish); close to the ground - *"He do hull that whully fleet."* he throws the quoit very close to the ground.

Fleeting Pan - huge shallow dish used for milk before separators.

Flepped - (skimmed) milk.

Flernecking - flaunting, ostentatious.

Flick - touch lightly. *"He flicked him with his whip."*

Flittermouse - bat

Flocky - a flocky rose is like "la France", whose petels are not compact.

Foky - spongy. *'a foky tarnip.'*

Forrerd - forward

For why - why.

Four-eyed - a person wearing spectacles.

Fourses - break for refreshments around mid-afternoon. Fourses cakes were baked for the afternoon break .

Fowt (Faut) - fault, possibly from the Dutch *fout*. *"He never found no fowt (faut) in his work".*

Fozy - unsound (of a hay crop).

Frail - rush dinner bag.

Frawry - stale, bad smelling.

Frazzle - to fray out; said of material.

Fresher / Fog Nightingale - Frog.

Frimicate - to speak affectedly.

Friz - frozen.

Froises - pancakes.

Frorn - frozen.

Frotting *(Essex)* - rubbing. (*Frotter* - to stroke.)

Frutter - old name for beachcomber; also poulterer.

Fudder - further.

Funk - dust.

Furnitude - furniture

Fustigation *(Essex)* - a beating.

Fyeing - *'fyeing out'* and *'bottom fyeing'* are terms used by hedgers and ditchers.

Gainer - more convenient.

Galder - coarse, vulgar.

Gander - To gad, ramble.

Gansey - Guernsey or Jersey made of wool.

Garnderin' - rambling in a meaningless way.

Garp - to stare with open mouth.

Gatly - troublesome. *"He was a gatly boy."*

Gavel, to - rake up barley into heaps ready for carting.

Gawk - lout.

Gelver - to throb. *"Ma tuth don't ache; but it kip gelverin'."*

Getting - going. *"I must be getting."*

Gimble - to grin or smile.

Gits - gains. *"My owd watch gits."*

Glose *(Essex)* - loose overshoes.

Gly-halter - a halter with winkers.

Golls - fat chops.

Gon - gave. *"He gon it me."* gave it to me.

Good Tidily - pretty well. *"How are you today?" "I'm good tidily thank ye."*

Goodish - a goodish few - a fair number.

Goodly tight - in tolerably good condition.

Goun *(Essex)* - given

Green, to - to strangle.

Greened - hanged.

Green Horse - *see 'Coltishness'.*

Gris *(Essex)* - marten (a costly fur).

Groops (Gripe) - runnels cut in land to take off surface water *Griping* or *re-grooping* his strip of land was once the obligation of each holder of land in the common field.

Groundsels *(Norfolk)* - foundations.

Grub - something to eat.

Grunny - the end of a pig's snout.

Gulsh - plump, souse, properly, into mud.

Hain - raise up, elevate.

Hain't - have not. *"I hain't finished yet."*

Handsome - beautiful. *"Ar'n't those flowers handsome?"*

Happen - perhaps.

Hark to - listen to.

Hather - instruction to a horse to turn left. *"Com' hather, Captain."*

Hatter - to harrass, exhaust.

Haysel - the haymaking season.

Head-Strike - climax of passion. *"Master went on the head-strike as ever I did hear."*

Heald *(Essex)* - pour out.

Heater piece - a triangular piece of ground, so called after the old fashioned three-cornered heaters used in the box iron.

Heel-in - to plant temporarily in the ground pending removal to its ultimate home.

Hefty weather - stormy.

Hem-gear - trace-horse's harness.

Hemplands - small pightles (enclosures of land) formerly used for growing hemp.

Hen's Noseful - a very small quantity.

Herb - plant with medicinal properties.

Het - heated. *"All het up."*

Hev - have.

Hewed - held up.

Hicken-kite - hopscotch.

Higgledy-Piggledy - auntidy.

Highlows - a covering for the foot and ankle too high to be called a shoe, too low to be called a boot. *A stranger once asked a local lad the depth of a run of water in Suffolk between Blyford and Wenhaston and was rather puzzled to be told: ' 'bout highlow deep.'*

Hike - hurry out.

Himp - to limp.

Hinder - here comes a dove. *"Hinder come a dow."*

Hungles - hinges.

Hinnus - henhouse.

Hip - fruit of the wild briar.

Hobby-lantern - a will-o'-the-wisp.

Hodmandod (Hodmedod) - snail, little hooded man.

Hog-over-high - leapfrog.

Holl - field ditch, possibly from the Dutch *hol.*

Homage - to greet. A short-sighted lady to her friend: *"if I don't homage you when I'm out a-walking, dew you homage me."*

Honeymoon Salad - *"Just lettice alone!"*

Hoppit *(Essex)* - enclosed piece of ground, square paddock near house.

Hoppity-poise - hesitating.

Horkey - Harvest Supper.

Horry Frost - hoar-frost.

Horse-needle - dragonfly

Hounce - the ornament of red and yellow worstead spread over the collars of horses in a team.

Housen - houses.

Howd - hold. *"Howd hard ther owd gal, while I git yer bridle on."*

Hukker - stammer.

Hull - to pitch, throw.

Hulloes - labourer's heavy boots.

Hully (Wholly) - *"That hully stammed me."*

Hummer - neigh as a horse does.

Hump - upset. *"enough to give you the hump."*

Hu *(rhymes with 'huff')* - out of line. *"That wall is on the hu."*

Hued - hoed. *"He hued, he wed, he sued."* he hoed, he weeded, he sowed.

Hutkin - little hat.

Hylding *(Essex)* - a youngster.

Idle - full of fun. *"Mary is very idle"*

Ig'orance - ignorance *"tha's har* (her) *ig'orance."*

Ig'orant - ignorant.

Ile Mill - oil-mill.

'I like myself very well' - meaning I am very well satisfied with my present position or state.

Illustraited *(accent on 'u')* - "Illustrated London News."

Incourse - of course.

Itude *(Essex)* - place.

Ivory - ivy.

Jack - a swelling on a horse's hock.

Jack (apple) - whole apple baked in pastry.

Jacob - a toad.

Jag - an indefinate quantity of hay, under a load.

Jane - twilled cotton.

Jew - grumbled, complained. *"he jew at me,"* *"he jawed at me."*

Jiffy-wit - fidgety person.

Jiggery-Pokery - a shady deal.

Jimmer - hinge.

Joice - joist.

Jounce - bounce *"jounce the baby about."*

Joram - a stone bottle in a wicker case.

Kady - a sun bonnet.

Kail - to throw, as a stone.

Keeler - large wooden tub used for making butter or beer.

Keeping-Room - the common parlour of a farmhouse. In Cambridge it is applied to an undergraduate's sitting-room.

Keys - ashen keys - the seed vessels of the ash tree.

Kindling - sticks used to 'lay' a fire.

Kitch - to catch.

Klyde - pocket.

Knap-kneed - knock-kneed.

Knobble - the outstanding crust on a loaf of bread.

Knubble - a small knob.

Lairy / Loopy - brainless

Lallop - a simpleton.

Lally-gags - straps worn round trouser legs.

Lam - to beat.

Largesse - a gift to harvesters.

Lashy - pulpy.

Learn - teach. *"he learn'd me to talk proper."*

Lessest - least.

Licked - beaten. *"He had him well licked long before the end."*

Lief - as soon. *"I'd as lief do one as the other."*

Ligger - a fish line with a flat, wooden float, for catching pike.

Likelys - *"Have they any money?" "Not likelys!"*

Likes - type of person. *"I shan't do it for the likes o' him."*

Limpsy (Limpy) - flabby

Lither Oaf *(Essex)* - wicked lout (slippery fellow).

Loblolly - a badly cooked fish.

Loke-way - an enclosed or sunken footpath.

Lollipops - sweetmeats.

Longmans *(accent on the 'a')* - "Longman's Magazine."

Lug - to move, drag. *"I lugged the heavy sacks to the barn."*

Luggersome - heavy. *"The roads are very luggersome."*

Main, in the - underdone.

Mank - mess up, spoil. *'This hay is manky'* poor quality, spoiled.

Mardle - a pond. also to gossip.

Mardling - gossiping. The village pond was once a meeting place for the women collecting water and the men watering their animals, hence the gossiping which took place took its name from the pond.

Marn't - may not.

Master - big and fine. *"That's a master plant."*

Master One - skilfull (at football).

Mawkin (Malkin) - scarecrow. or a sluvenly dressed woman.

Mawther (Mother) - young girl.

Meese (Meesen) - mice.

Mersh - marsh.

Met - mate, pal.

Middlin - quite well. *"I,m feelin' middlin today."*

Minefer - a stoat.

Miser'ble - miserable, tiresome *"Oh those miser'ble (church) bells.*

Misfaced - a misfaced crist - defaced armorial shield.

Misturnment *(Essex)* - perversion.

Mite - in the smallest degree *"She's not altered a mite."*

Mizzle - misty drizzle.

Mobbed - abused, scalded. *"I gave him a good mobbin'."* Used as good-natured teasing: *"Mr. Groome do mob me so."*

Moise - to mend, improve, thrive, increase (in growth) as a plant.

Moking - crossing and recrossing. *"I kept moking across the road to find a clean path.*

Mole-country - the graveyard.

Mopsy-wopsy - drunk.

Morgered (Mortgaged) - destroyed *"rabbits have morgered the carnations."*

Mow - a scythe.

Mowld *(rhymes with 'howled')* - mould *"mowldy cheese."*

Muck-sweat (Muck-wash) - to perspire. *"I'm all of a muck-sweat."*

Mud-barges - thick boots.

Muddlins - not worth much. *"he's amongst the muddlins."*

Mumping - carol singing.

Munging - a good feed.

Musheroom - mushroom.

Musicioners - musicians.

Nannick / Nannock - Idling, larking around. *"She wus nannockin' 'stead o' dewin' har wark."*

Nattle - to be bustling, stirring about trifles.

Natural - national *"Do they go to the British or the Natural School?"*

Nawthen' - nothing

Neat-House - how-house.

Neesen - nest.

Never - did not look. *"he never looked"*

Nib *(Essex)* - short for Isabel.

Nigh nor by - near. *"He nivva com' nigh nor by us nowadays."*

Ninarias *(Essex)* - nonsense. (Ninny - an idiot).

'Nip over' - I will come and see you. *"I will nip over to see you."*

Noar's ark - a cloud resembling a large overturned boat.

Noddle - head or nape (of the neck)

Nonce - for the once.

No Matters - not at all well. *"He is no matters today."*

Nowty - naughty.

Nut - head.

Oaten - cutting oats. *"He is gone oaten."*

Offer (Orfer) - offer up, submit.

Old Tom Shock - a village ghost.

Old Scrile - a withered old person.

'On to you' - ask or remind you. *"I shall be on to you again when I see you."*

Ort - or *"take that last cake, ort I will."*

Orts - scraps.

Ouches *(Essex)* - jewels.

'Out - without, except.

Owd - old. It may come from *oud* the Dutch word for old.

Pair o' Beads - a necklace. Survival of an old term found in ancient wills denoting a rosary.

Pakenose Lollapers *(Norfolk)* - people with excessive curiousity.

Pa'ment - pavement

Parky - nippy, cold weather. *"It's real parky out today."*

Ped - a hamper with a lid, a fowl-basket.

Pennes *(Essex)* - feathers.

Pet - upset, in a paddy.

Pightle - small enclosure of land generally adjoining or near a dwelling. The term is usually applied to the small fields constituting a small farm holding or tenancy and a two-pightle farmer is a contemptuous designation of a small farmer. *(see Hemplands).*

Pingy - fastidious and difficult to please about his food.

Pin o' the throat - uvula.

Pipin - small, deformed pig.

Plancke - *(from the French plancher).* thick floor board.

Poachy - boggy.

Podgy - thick 'podgy porridge'.

Popple - poplar tree

Possessed - occupied by an evil spirit *"the child fared wholly possessed."*

Posy - nosegay.

Pot-ladles - tadpoles.

Pow - paw.

Power - much *"he did me a power of good."*

Prame - flat-bottomed boat or lighter.

Precious - very. *"He did precious little to help them."*

Preux *(Essex)* - brave *(French)*

Proper - smart *"tha's proper."*

Pulk - a muddy hole or pond.

Pummer - a large one. *"That's a pummer!"*

Push - a boil.

Purely - very well in health.

Puskets - pea-pods.

Putter About - to work casually and indiscriminately.

Quackle - to choke. *"Quackled ta dead."* (choked to death).

Quick - hawthorn, may.

Quinchling (Squinchling) - a small apple.

Quoddle - to boil gently.

Rabs - large feet. *(see 'Trilbys')*

Raffling pole - for stirring the ashes in ovens.

Rafty *(pronounced 'rarfty')* - foggy or nippy, cold weather.

Rally - to sift.

Rannie / Ranny - shrew/vole.

Ranter - a can to carry beer from cellar to cup.

Rear - rare (underdone) meat. Rear hay - hay not thoroughly made and still partly green.

Reckon - to think or believe. *"I reckon that it will be so."*

Refty - raw day.

Releet - roads that meet at the same point.

Riddled - rather a riddle. *"it's rather riddled."*

Riled (Roiled) - angry. *"I'm wholly riled"* - very angry.

Ringes - ridges.

Ringle - to ringle the pigs - to put rings in their snouts.

Rip - imp or naughty child.

Risty - rusty, stale *"the pork's tarn'd risty."*

Rit - wart.

Roarer - a broken-winded horse.

Rocky - unsound.

Roger's blast *(Norfolk)* - a sudden gusty wind or whirlwind.

Roke - fog.

Romant - romance.

Roment - to raise a report or falsehood.

Rose - of watering-can used in gardens.

Rove - the scab of a sore.

Row - raw.

Ruff - roof.

Runned - ran.

Sall / Sarah - a hare.

Sapy - unhealthy look.

Sars-a-mine - exclamation of surprise. What is the meaning of this?

Sauce - any kind of green vegetable.

Sawney - soft, foolish. *"He wore a sawney, he wore."*

Say of it - taste of it.

Scant - sly person.

Schisms - fancies. Said to a child *"none o' yer schisms."*

Scoot - an irregular angle.

Scorfum - dinner

Scour - wash thoroughly.

Scrab - to rush . *"I had to scrab to get the bus."*

Scrab - to scratch, selfish, grasping.

Scran - food.

Scranched - scratched.

Scrog-footed - describing a person who walks *'like a duck'* - heel in and toes out.

Scruffy - half-torn.

Sculp - to scoop out.

Sele (OE: Seal) - Time or season: Haysel, Barley-seal.

Seed-maund - a basket used for holding the seed when it was sown broadcast.

Seft - saved or laid it by for you. *"I seft it for you"*

Sensible - I could not make him understand it. *"I could not make him sensible on it."*

Sere - dry. said of wood.

Several - many *"Are there many blackberries about this year?"* *"There are several about."* (a non-committal reply.)

Sew - sowed *"I sew that seed."*

Sextant - sexton

A newspaper cutting of January 5th 1895 related to a story which appeared in the 'Church Times' :

A tripper, meditating among the tombs in an East Anglian churchyard, seeing a venerable individual at work among the graves, said "I suppose, my man, you are one of the officials of this church?" "Ficials, sir? Why, lawk; I hardly know what I deu be! When Parson Smith come, he say I were a sextant. And then Parson Jones he come, and he fare to call me the beetle (beadle), and now Muster Rob'son be our parson, and he say I'm the vargin (verger)."

Shail - to move loosely.

Shanny - wayward, headstrong, high-spirited. *"She was so shanny."*

Sharming *(Norfolk)* - crying, making a noise.

Shew *(rhymes with new)* - showed.

Ship - sheep. Invariably inland public houses called The Ship Inn refer to sheep and not the maritime vessel.

Shoaf (Shuf) - sheaf.

Shottenheron - a thin, gawky person.

Shruck - shrieked.

Shutting-in time *(Norfolk)* - sunset.

Shy - a small, partly open, shed.

Sight - many. *"There was a great sight of them."* meaning there were a great many of them.

Sizzle - shrivel up and hiss. *"I put it on the fire and heard it sizzle".*

Skaffel - a straight-bladed spade.

Skeedaddle - run away.

Skewbald (pony) - irregularly marked with white and brown or red.

Skinker - one who serves drinks.

Skupput - shovel

Slant - a sly person

Sleep Abroad - be buried. *"I shall soon hev to sleep abroad now"* (in the churchyard).

Slither - split lengthways.

Slop - shirtlike garment worn over shirt to keep it clean whilst ditching.

Slub - mud.

Sluggy - small-built.

Slug-horned - crumple-horned (of a cow).

Slurrop - to swallow with noise.

Smacked - to dash. *"He smacked in arter me."* meaning "He dashed in after me."

Smallen - to make smaller, of a garment.

Smur - drizzle. *"tha's a smurrin' with rain."*

Snarth - a catch or snag in a tale that is told.

Snack - *"give us a snack o' that pudden'"* meaning to give a small piece of pudding.

Snack *(Norfolk)* - latch (of a door).

Snake-berries - berries of the White Bryony

Snasty - ill-tempered.

Sneed - shaft or pole of a scythe.

Sneerchap - a sarcastic person.

Snew - snowed.

Snick - to snip or cut along the edge of paper or cloth to make it adjust itself to a curve.

Snotty-Gobbles - yew berries.

Snug, to - to pet, cuddle.

Soaker - earthen pan for flower pot.

Soothly stirred *(Essex)* - persuaded.

Sondy - a sandy-haired person.

Soul - person. *"She's a good little soul."*

Spank - to move swiftly and stoutly.

Sparrer-grass - asparagus.

Sperket - a hat peg.

Splod - walk heavily.

Spuffle - hurried or flustered.

Squat - hidden or quiet. *"He knows all about it, but he's the one to keep it squat."*

Squiny - squinting.

Squit - twaddle, nonsense. *"When he gets fuddled with drink he allus talks a load o' squit."*

Stain of the Blood - related to. *"I've a stain o' the blood with her."*

Stam - to astonish.

Stammed - utterly astonished. *"That wholly stammed me."*

Stiddle - bedstead.

Stingy - spiteful. A child who pinches another is told not to be so stingy.

Stoun - to long for.

Stover - clover, used as winter cattle-feed.

Stulps - post, stump.

Sturrings - small household jobs.

Suckers - sweetmeats.

Suss - pigwash or to drink noisily.

Sustren *(Essex)* - sisters.

Sve *(Essex)* - follow.

Swale - a low place, shade.

Swangways - half tipsy.

Swarm - to climb a tree with arms and legs.

Sweven *(Essex)* - dreams.

Swift - newt.

Swimmer - Norfolk dumpling.

Swobble - to spill over.

Sybbit - banns. *"They had thar sybbits ast at church."*

Take in - turn (to the right, etc.)

Tater-Trap - a large mouth - possibly from potato trap. *"Jest yew shut yer tater trap, bor."*

Teetortum - a see-saw.

Tempest - thunderstorm.

Thaking - thatching.

Theayter *(accent on 'ay')* - theatre.

'There 't be' - there it is.

Thewis *(Essex)* - manners.

Threats of Corporal Punishment - *"I'll larn him." "I'll warm his jacket." "I'll give it him." "I'll give him what for." "I'll give him a rare hidin'." "I'll flee* (flay) *him."*

Thumb-piece - a labourer's lunch in the field; as much as the hand holds without the aid of a plate.

Thrummer - threepenny piece.

Tidy - very, pretty. *"It is tidy cheap."*

Tiffle about - do little light jobs.

Tight - big. *"good tight bit o' green."*
Tightly good - thoroughly.
Timber-Hill - staircase. said to a child at bedtime *"Time to climb timber-hill."* *"Up Timber-Hill, down of Sheet Lane, and anchor in Blanket Bay."*
Time Tables - Seeds of the Dandelion
Ting - to strike a key on metal to collect a swarm of bees; *'to ting bees.'*
Tip-sluff - wooden scooplike tool used in ditching.
Tisick - cough.
Tite up - to make tidy. *"I've tited them all up."*
Tittery - weak in the body.
'Titty Bit, a, and a Doddy Mite' - a very small piece.
Tod - 28 pounds of wool.
Together - several people. *"You've got a nice day today, together."* or for emphasis *"Now then, you together."* or *"Where be you a-goin' all alone, together?"*
Tol de rol - drunkenness.
Tommin' Double - a ploughing term.
To on them - two of them.
Torent *(Essex)* - a town.
Torment - foment *"I'm a-gooin' to torment that 'ere ship (sheep)."*
Totty - small.
Trape - walking wearily. *"She come a traping through the mud."*
Trashed *(Norfolk)* - *"we trashed (thrashed) the corn."*
Trickey - shy.
Trilbys - small ladylike feet.
Tritel - to throw as when pitching a steel quoit.
Tumbril (Tumbrell) - hay waggon.
Tunder - tinder.
Twiddle - a small pimple.
Twizzle round - turn round, reverse.
Ugsome *(Essex)* - ugly.
Unawars - unawares.
Uncili *(Essex)* - unhappy.
Un-Dead-Liness *(Essex)* - immortality.
Undern *(Essex)* - 11 o'clock (9 o' clock).
Unkivered - uncovered. *To kiver* - to cover.
Unsensed - rendered insensible.
Up o' the Hill - up the hill.
Vapouring - fidgeting.
Varmit (Varmin) - vales or vailes. money given to servants.
Vexed - grieved, sorry. *"I was vexed when I saw how ill he was looking."*

Walberswick whisperer - a loud-voiced native of walberswick (Suffolk). *"Yow ma' har him oova t' Sowle* (Southwold).*"*

Warldathowtind - (world without end). never done. *'Thar's warldathowtind thar'*, in reference to some long, tedius, endless task.

Walk - a garden path.

Wallop - to flog. *'A woman, a dog and a walnut tree,*
the more you wallop 'em the better they'll be.'

Walter - to roll, as laid corn on the ground.

Waps - wasp.

Waspy (Warspy) - angry.

Waste, to - diminish, shrink.

Watering - a ford.

W'a's this? - what is this?

Wayzgoose or Waygoose - an entertainment given by a master printer to his workmen about Bartholomew-tide (24th August).

Weather-Breeder - *"This is a weather-breeder."* used of a time of unseasonable weather.

Well-happed - fortunate.

Wemme - spot, blemish, fault. *"Tha's a fine cairpit; 't ain't got a wem in ut, nowhere."*

Went - gone. *"If she'd a-known as how she couldn't a-went she'd a-writ you a letter."*

Whistler - a broken-winded horse that breathes hard with a shrill sound.

Whiteness *(Essex)* - turning road.

Whittle - make smaller.

Why-wiffles - fidgets. *'He can't kip still; he got the why-wiffles.'*

Winnick - to cry weakly. *"She winnicks so."*

Witches *(Suffolk)* - cockchafers (may beetle)

Wobble - to wrap untidily. *'He wobbled that parcel up anyhow.'*

Woosh - instruction to a horse to turn right.

Worn't - Wasn't.

Wuzzling - falling. *'He com' wuzzlin' down ta stairs.'*

Other examples of the accent put on an unusual syllable are:
Deficit - *accent on first 'i';* Hereditary - *accent on the 'a';* Relatives - *accent on the 'a'.*

In the following words the vowels or diphthong is rounded as the 'u' in 'puss' quite different from the 'u' in 'fuss' : both, cooper, open, post, roof, room, soup, spoon, stone, stoop, toast. *We turn 'ow' into 'er' in :* arrow, follow, widow, window. Loft becomes *lorft* and office becomes *orfice.*

Nautical Words & Phrases

Bad Bread - *"Come to bad bread".* to come off worse.

Bawly-Boat - a large yawl-like boat used for salwaging purposes; swiping for anchors, etc.

Bean - *"To throw in a bean."* to put in one's oars - throw in an objection or, as an old-fashioned farmer's wife was overheard to say to her husband relating to an ill-advised marriage of her son's: *"Joe, bor, you must hull in an obistacle."*

Blind Sail - a sail that hangs so low as to blind the steersman to his course.

Blow-off - to brag, boast. also as in *"Well, if they'd call'd on me, I'd a' blown off a song like the rest."*

Bobbing Joan - Jetsum. Wreckage continually coming up to the surface then disappearig again.

Brown-Herring - a herring slightly cured for speedy use and home consumption.

Bowse - to apply tackles. *"We bowsed it up from the bottom."*

Brot-Tow - scraps and fragments of rope collected to make coarse paper. An old fellow used to go by the name of *'Old Brawtoe'* among the beachmen because of his dealings in this line.

Brustle - a compound of bustle and rustle. *"Why, the old girl brustle along like a hedge-sparrow!"* said of a round-bowed vessel spuffling through the water.

Bull - *"He know no more of Herrin'-drivin' than a bull does of a Sunday."* *"He spuffled about 'till he 'sweat like a bull'."*

'Butter a Cat's Paws' - a charm resorted to to attach a cat to the house.

Butterfly - considered lucky and therefore treated tenderly if it strays into house or net-chamber.

Caravan-Hat - old-fashioned poke-bonnet or the later tilt of a covered cart.

Coach; Coached - out of pocket. *"I'm coach'd."* or *"I'm coach."*

Chopp'd Hay - smuggled tobacco.

Company Keepers - ships that sail together as well as lovers who 'walk' together. *"That owd Jemina and Woilet (Violet) are rare company-keepers."*

Crabb *(believed to be unique to Southwold)* - a fisherman's capstan.

Dee - *"Steady as a dee (die?)"* *"That old girl fared right silly at first, but, when we got into deep water, went as steady as a dee."*

Double Tides - double work. George Crabbe ends a poem concerning a thrifty but unpenurious couple in their little farm:

> *". . Thus both, that waste itself might work in vain,*
> *Wrought double-tides, and all was well again."*

Fake - to take or catch.

Flip-Flop - the alternate flapping of the sails from side to side.

Flurries - sudden, and partial commotions of the sea, as over a shoal. *"I never* To *knew the say* (sea) *in such a takin'; all flurries like."*

Foul - *"When I get foul of those nets."* take them in hand to repair.

Force-put - forced. *"I didn't till I was right force-put to it."*

Frapp - a crowd, crush. *"There's a pretty frap of luggers down about the Humber, I warrant."*

Frothy - too light on the water (a vessel) as from insufficient ballast. *"Come a breeze, the old girl would blow away like a thistle-blossom."*

Friday - by some, a change of weather - even from bad to better - is looked for on a Friday.

Gansy - fisherman's blue sweater.

Gast-cope - *"going gast-cope"* without hire or pay, as a boy on his first trial voyage.

Gingerbread Gilt - the gloss of fancy or preference. *"He's a fine fellow with his new business now; but, once come a kink in the rope, it'll soon knock the gilt off the gingerbread."* Gingerbread is also an ornamental carving or guilding about a ship's bows.

'Good as Gold' - is a good thing but *"good as old gold"* is better.

Gowry - greedy, voracious.

Grace - *"Laid up in Grace"* or *"Laid up in Lavender".* away from common use.

Home - *"At home."* in one's right wits.

Hot - *"Tides run hot just now in the sailor's eye",* a double-portentous phenomenon when *'like a sluice'* or *'like a soldier's horse'.*

Herrin' Spink - The golden-crested wren often caught by the hand while *latching* in the rigging or among the gear during North Sea fishing.

Hues - *Old Hues,* the tan water in which nets have already been soaked.

Half-and-Half - the Lugger which operated on the principle of the crew and owner sharing the profits.

In-bred - *"He wouldn't take off a halfpenny* (discount) *today; but offered to take off sixpence in the pound next month, when the stuff'll be eighteen pence dearer. That's in-bred work, I call it."*

Ivory - *"The wind sprung up, and the sea began to show his ivory."*

Joop - *"When those Penzance men see us go out on a Sunday, lord how they would joop and hallor after us."*

Kicklin'-string - on which a warp of herrings is carried, hung through the gills.

Kids - the compartments on deck on which herrings are stowed.

Laig - a chasm in the cliff at Hopton, Suffolk, running from the village to the sea.

Last-come-Last - At last *"the old gentleman fared long upon the drope, and, last come last, give way altogether."*

Manor - *"The ship was wrecked upon the Manor."* stranded above the ebb, to which the Lord of the Manor's right extends. And if a vessel not only strike, but go to pieces there, he claims a fee from the owner. Think of that last drop in the cup!

66

be wrecked, half drowned oneself and one's ship quite lost, and then have to pay a fee for the privilege of her knocked to pieces where she lies!

Macaroni - a fore-and-aft schooner without square yards.

Mother - when a Lugger does so well that another is built out of her profits she is said to be *Mother* of the new one.

Mote - a vessel in size between a Coble and a Keel.

New Moon - when first seen (but not through glass), be sure to turn your money over in your pocket by way of making it grow there.

Norsel - attached to drift nets made by twine-spinners.

Old Bones - *"That child'll never make Old Bones."* live to be old.

Pencil-work - *"His room is swept as clean as pencil-work."*

Pinch - when the falling tide has left its mark on the sand or shingle it is said to have pinched.

Pup - any undersized thing.

Puff the Gaff - to blow a secret. *"He thought to get clear off but his mate puffed the gaff and they were soon after him."*

Punt - the Lowestoft lug-sailed longshore boat.

Range - swell of the sea. *"There's a terrible range into the harbour when the wind blow strong from the south."*

Ride to Wind - When in the slack, or lack, of tide, a vessel rides head to wind at her anchor. She is then *'wind-rode'*.

Rips and Trucks - odds and ends; fragments.

Rooms - The spaces between a boat's thwarts thus divided and named: 1 Fore-peak; 2 Fore-room; 3 Well; 4 After-room

Roomly - roomy *"a good roomly boat, she."*

Rockstaff - such yarn as old wives spin *"so I've heard say."*

Rover - a *slink*, ill-conditioned codfish.

Run-in - treat us to. *"Well, mate, how much do you run us in tonight?"*

Red Gaps - The master boat among the luggers, she that has raised most money by the voyage, distinguishes her crew with red caps in token of victory.

Ruther - rudder.

Samson-Post - The pedestal-post of the mast from deck to keelson.

Scare - To *'get the scare'* seems to mean *'give* the scare'. *"He was best man at first, but 'tother get the scare of him in the end."*

Scram - odds and end, and leavings of victuals.

Scutcheons - wooden baskets shaped somewhat between butcher's trays and coal-scuttles with handles atop, to carry *fresh* herring.

Services - Pieces of old lint, spun yarn, wrapped round rope or warp to prevent its chafing.

Shake cap - Another form of 'Pitch and Toss'.

Skeet - To skim the surface.

Skulter - porpoise.

Shottener - a shotten herring.

Smell the ground - A vessel loses the control of her helm in proportion as she nears the ground; and so is said '*to smell it*'.

Shimmer - Not only the glitter of fish coming out of the water *on*-deck, but of the *safer* of fish itself.

Slite - Wear and tear. *"That fore-sail have had a deal of slite this last winter."*

Smolt - A calm. *"It fell to a smolt towards evening."*

Stove down - *"There was an old gannet a-watchin' us aloft; so I threw him a mackerel: he turn'd his old eye upon it, and stove down and clean'd him off in a wink."*

Sprat's eye - a sixpence.

Thole - The peg, between two of which the oar works.

Three-sticker - Salwagee for any three-masted ship; thrice blest, if she be, or promise to be, in trouble.

Tom Tailor - By this name is Mother carey's chicken known in these seas.

Trim-Tram - The Yarmouth fore-and-aft longshore fishing boat.

Truck - Any sort of cap, or '*tile*' for the head.

'Turn like a top' - *'Turn like a fish'* - said of any vessel that comes handily round, does not linger in stays, etc.

Twine-masking - The cord by which the net is attached to the *norsels*, the *norsels* being attached to the outer cord of all, called the *net-rope*.

Weep - The nails weeping with rust is one sign of the ship's *complaining*.

Wings - The separated sides of the lugger's hold, in which the fish are stowed.

Wind-proud - A cloud big with wind.

Weasel - A small buoy fastened at such a depth to the vessel's anchor as only to show above the low water of a Spring tide.

Many of our shipping terms have a Dutch origin; here are a few samples:

clipper - klipper; **yawl** - jol; **frigate** - fregat; **sail** - zeil; **mast** - mast; **boom** - boom; **deck** - dek; **anchor** - anker; **cable** - touw; **to tow** - touwen; **luff** - loef; **ship's swab** - scheep's schrobber *(pronounced scrobber)*; **ship's biscuit** - scheep's beschuit.

East Anglian Bird Names

Bald coot - Coot
Bank Swallow - Sandmartin
Bar Goose / Burrow Duck - Sheldrake
Barley-Bird - Nightingale.
Blackcap - Marsh tit
Bottle-bump - Bittern
Butcher Bird - Red backed shrike
Cob - Great crested grebe
Daw / Kaddaw / Caddow - Jackdaw
Devaton / Develin / Screecher - Swift or Swallow.
Dow *(rhymes with 'how')* - Dove or Pigeon.
Dun-Billy - Crow.
Dunnock, Hedge-Betty, Hedge-grubber, Spurrer - Hedge Sparrow
Felfet, Fulfer - Fieldfare
Fire Tail - Redstart
Gowk - Cuckoo
Harnser / Harnsie - Heron
Herrin' Spink - Golden-crested wren
Hock / Windhover - Hawk or Kestrel
Horned Owl - Long eared owl
Hornipies - Peewits
Jilly-hooter - Owl
Kentishmen - Hooded crows
King Harry - Goldfinch
Kittywren / Tityrene - Common wren.
Lavrock - Skylark
Mavis - Thrush
Madge - Magpie
Missler - Missel thrush
Mussel Catcher - Oyster catcher
Nettle Creeper - Whitethroat
Olph, Blood Olp, Red Olph, Nope - Bullfinch
Oushatt / Oushie Doo - Woodpigeon
Ovenbird, Ground-oven, Hayjack - Willow warbler, Willow wren, Whitethroat
Peeweep - Green plover
Penny Wagtail / Polly Dishwasher - Pied wagtail
Pool Snipe - Redshank
Pudding Poke / Bottle Tit - Long-tailed Tit.

Reed Pheasant - Bearded tit
Ruddock - Robin
Saw Sharpener - Great tit
Sea Mew - Common gull
Sea Swallow - Common tern
Snake Bird - Wryneck
Southwold-crows - Seagulls
Spink / Pettychaps - Chaffinch
Stone Runner - Ringed plover
Sturnel - Starling
Thicknee - Stone curlew
Titlark - Meadow pipit
Wallbird / Beambird - Spotted flycatcher.
Whew Duck - Wigeon
Woodcock Owl - Short eared owl
Woodsprite / Yaffle Rainbird - Green woodpecker
Yulla-hammant - Yellow hammer

East Anglian Flower Names

A-kiss-behind-the-garden-gate, Jack-at-the-garden-gate, Three-faces-under-a-hood - Pansy, Heartsease
Barber's Brushes, Brushes and Combs - Teasel, Dipsacus
Bear's Ears - Polyanthus
Bird's Eye - Germander Speedwell
Blackguard's Friend - Polygonatum Multiflorum *(heals bruises after fighting)*
Boar-thistle - Cotton Thistle
Bread and Cheese - Mallow
Bull's-Eye Daisies, Christy Anthem, May Daisies, Moon Daisies, Ox-Eyed Daisies - Chrysanthemum.
Bunweed Buns - Black Knapweed
Butter and Eggs - Narcissus
Come Haste-to-the-Wedding - Rock Cress, Alyssum
Cow-mumble - Hogweed
Cupid's Locket - The Lyre Flower, Dielytra
Daffy-down-dilly - Daffodil
Drunken Men - Caltha Palustris.
Fair Maid of February - Galanchus Nivalis.
Fat Hen - White Goosefeet

Fiddle-sticks - Water Figwort
Fitches - vetch, climbing plant.
Five-fingers - Oxlip
Garland Flower, Cornelian - Mezereon, Spurge Laurel
Gill-go-on-the-ground, Runaway Jack - Ground Ivy
Ginger - Tansy
Goslings - Palm blossom
Grandfather Greybeard - Wild Clematis
Guttrich - Dogwood
Gutweed - Corn Sow-thistle
Gypsy-rhubarb - Burdock
Hogknife or Huntsman's Cap - Iris
Hundred-leafer - Green Gravel, Milfoil
Jacob's Ladder - Common Gladiolus
Jam-tarts - Willow Herb
Jimrainams, Soldiers' Buttons, Stinking Bob - Geraniums, (Robertianum)
John-go-to-bed-at-noon - Goat's Beard
King-cups - Marsh Marigold
King's Cup, Marsh Marigolds - Caltha Palustris.
Lady's Bonnets - Dove Flower, Columbine
Lady's Fingers - Kidney Vetch
Lady's Frock - Cuckoo Flower
Ladies'-hair - Quaking-grass
Lambs' Tails - Hazel catkins
Lords and Ladies - Arum
Mary Bud's, Gold Cups - Buttercup
Milkmaids - Meadow Bitter Cress
Miser's Shillings, Ready Money - Honesty
Nathan-driving-his-chariot - Monkshood
New Year's Gift - Winter Aconite
Nipnoses - Snapdragon
None-so-Pretty, Pretty Betsy - Saxifraga Umbrosa.
Paigle, Payles (Peegles) - Cowslip. "Jaundice ha' torn him yulla as a paigle."
Pickpocket - Shepherd's Purse
Pigs' tootles - Birds'-foot Trefoil
Piney *(long 'i')* - Peony.
Queen Anne's Needlework, None-so-Pretty, Sweet Betsy - London Pride
Rattle-jack - Yellow Lousewort
Red Hot Poker - Torch Lily
Sention - Groundsel

Shepherd's sundial, Shepherd's weather-glass - Scarlet Pimpernel

Shirt-buttons - Stitchwort

Snakes - Campion

Soloman's Seal - Polygonatum Multiflorum.

Suckling - white clover.

Sweet Betsy - Valerian

Sweethearts - Cleavers

The Fortune Teller, What's o'clock - Dandelion

Traveller's Joy - Clematis

Wire-weed - Knot-grass, Common hedge mustard (Norfolk)

Witchgrass - Perennial Rye-grass
